CONTENTS

ABOUT THE AUTHOR

Aisling Mackey is the creator and owner of several online businesses, which between them have served over 18,000 customers, including:

- www.craftsupplies.ie: Ireland's biggest online crafting store.

- www.diywedding.ie: a website for DIY wedding stationery and accessories.

- www.diyinvites.ie: invitation kits and party supplies for all party occasions, from birthdays to anniversaries and communions.

- www.budgetwedding.ie: an information portal site that contains articles and information on how to save money on your wedding.

Aisling has a 1st class honours degree in Computer Science from University College Dublin, and spent eight years working in the computer industry, including several years in the USA. She has a young son, Luke, and lives in Dublin.

CLICKTHROUGH

A Practical Guide to Starting a
Successful Internet Business

Aisling Mackey

Published by
OAK TREE PRESS
19 Rutland Street, Cork, Ireland
www.oaktreepress.com

© 2010 Aisling Mackey

A catalogue record of this book is
available from the British Library.

ISBN 978 1 904887 38 6

Although the author and publisher have taken every care to ensure
that the information published in this book is correct at the time of
going to press, neither can take any responsibility for any loss or
damage caused to any person as a result of acting on, or refraining
from acting on, any information published herein. Professional advice
should be obtained before entering into any legally binding
commitments.

TABLES

FIGURES

1
INTRODUCTION

The world that is the Internet is many things to many people. It is at once a library, a window to all the shops in the world, a research tool, a social meeting point, a place to file your taxes and to register your child for school. Its resources and power are endless and, at times, awesome.

Taming the World Wide Web to produce your own Internet business can appear an insurmountable task, doable only by the technical savants of the world. So much terminology and technical knowledge seems to be required, it's an uphill battle just to become familiar with the components alone, while building your own business can seem nigh on impossible.

This book is designed to offer a practical step-by-step guide to setting up your own online business, making it successful, and keeping it that way. It will cover a wide range of topics – from evaluating your business idea, to bringing it online, marketing it, and making it 'sticky' to keep customers interested month-on-month and to ensure continued success. Getting up and running may seem the hard part, but the Internet is a fast-paced, fickle and constantly-evolving environment. Continually attracting customers, keeping ahead of competitors and maintaining a loyal customer base is often the hardest part of running a successful online business.

My aim for this book is to demystify the whole process of setting up an Internet business and to provide practical advice, based on what

I have learned directly from building my own websites and businesses.

So let's start.

1.1 INTERNET BUSINESS MODELS

Our first port of call is to take a look at the various Internet business models in use on the web today. Nearly all business ideas are suited to using the Internet – the question is 'In what capacity?'. Should the Internet be used as a direct selling tool? As a marketing brochure? Is the business model for your idea designed to market a different kind of product – a service, a directory or a community model? The options are wider than you think when it comes to doing business on the Internet.

Below are examples of common Internet e-business models that use the Internet successfully. This list, though not exhaustive, shows most of the e-business models in use today:

- Online merchant selling tangible goods.
- Online merchant selling virtual / downloadable goods.
- Online brochure.
- Information portal.
- Directory of products / services.
- Social portal.
- Blog.
- Selling a service online.

The first and most obvious Internet business model is to use the web as a direct sales tool as an **online merchant selling tangible goods**, such as books, clothes or gadgets. This is the classic Amazon model, where the business is a shop and the shop-front is its website. Products or services are purchased directly through the website and then delivered through the post to the customer. The start and end of the customer interaction is all through the website, with no visit to a bricks and mortar outlet.

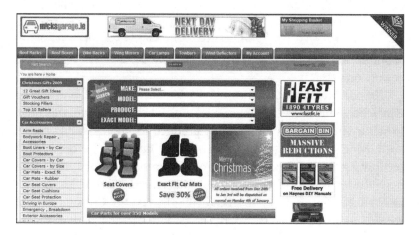

Figure 1.1: MicksGarage.ie: an online merchant selling tangible goods

Figure 1.2: Giftmaster.ie: another online merchant selling tangible goods

Online grocery shopping (Superquinn.ie or Tesco.ie) is another good example of this model, and there are many niche online shops doing extremely well in this area, too – such as baby clothes, online gift stores, flowers or toys. This is by far the most well-known occurrence of e-business on the web, and is what most people mean when talking about an Internet business. This will also be the area we focus most heavily on in this book.

The second internet business model, similar to the first, is to also be a merchant and to use the Internet as a direct sales tool but, this time, to **sell a virtual, or downloadable, product**. Examples of this model are buying music from iTunes, ebooks, or buying your computer's security software (such as McAfee, Norton) online, and then downloading directly onto your computer or mobile device. In this case, no shipping is done, no stock inventory needed. Customers often require more customer support, since downloading and installing software onto your computer is not as easy as accepting a parcel at your front door.

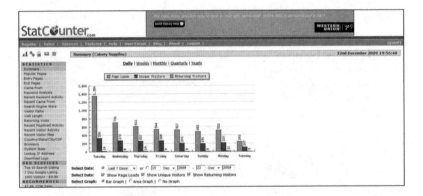

Figure 1.3: StatCounter: selling a virtual, or downloadable, product

Ebooks are another product that fit this virtual model. The ebook market, which has really taken off in very recent years with the success of Amazon's Kindle and Sony's E-Reader, while not popular for all readers or book types, has particular relevance for business or reference books. Such books provide expertise that is not readily available on Google, and which may be often searched for answers, quotes or information – making them perfect for buying and keeping in soft copies rather than hard. And, among travellers on the go, already there is a very definite market for what are essentially book versions of iPods, and it is likely only to grow. In addition, the continued rivalry between Sony and Amazon, both attempting to capture the e-reader market, has led to revised versions of the hardware coming out rapidly and improving with each iteration.

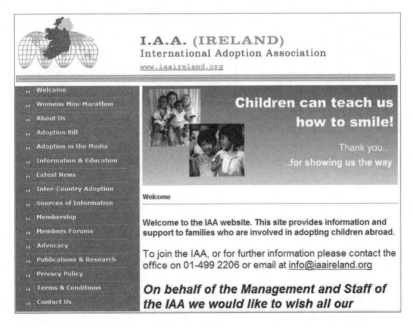

Figure 1.4: International Adoption Association: an online brochure

The third, and most common, model is to use the Internet as a marketing tool or **online brochure** for your business – to help customers to find you, to attract customers to your products, to educate them on what you provide, and to lead them to the next step in the sales process, whether this is to contact a sales person, order a catalogue or request information from you. In this case, the website is part of the sales process, but the customer must interact with the business outside of the web environment – on the phone or by visiting a store – in order to complete the sales process.

A fourth and increasingly common business model for the Internet is to provide a website which is an **information portal** or information centre in a particular domain or topic of interest. This type of website is also called an **infomediary.**

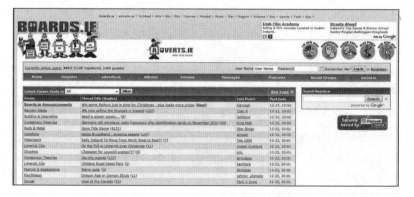

Figure 1.5: Boards.ie: an infomediary

The portal's focus may be weddings, music, sport, children / motherhood, crafts or a multitude of other human interests. An example of a good information portal in Ireland is **www.myhome.ie**. It provides a comprehensive listing of properties for sale, but also a plethora of advice and guides around buying property as well.

A web portal presents information
from diverse sources in a unified way.
Wikipedia

Another example of an infomediary is www.ireland.com, which has branched away from *The Irish Times* (though it is still owned by the group) to provide an Irish portal where you can book a trip or restaurant, read a blog or catch up on the news.

Figure 1.6: Ireland.com: a portal

In the portal business model, the website owner typically provides a large number of informational resources on the topic, such as news feeds, articles, chat room, blog, message forum and expert advice, and thus encourages a high number of visitors to the site from a particular demographic.

For all portals, the goal is to find and capture an audience, encouraging them to visit the site on a daily basis. Using the number of visitors to the site, the owner then can encourage product and service providers interested in reaching that audience to **advertise** on his / her site for a fee. Thus they can create an accompanying services directory providing, for example, a directory of sports shops and clubs on a sports portal. The fee charged to suppliers advertising in the directory is sometimes an annual subscription, and sometimes per-click-based. Thus the main revenue stream in this business model comes from **advertising**, and the 'product' offered to visitors is simply information.

A fifth model, similar to the fourth, is to provide just a **directory of products or services** in a particular area – without additional information such as articles or a forum. Since the customer is seeking a product or service in a particular domain, they will use this directory to find it. Directories of this kind are increasingly common.

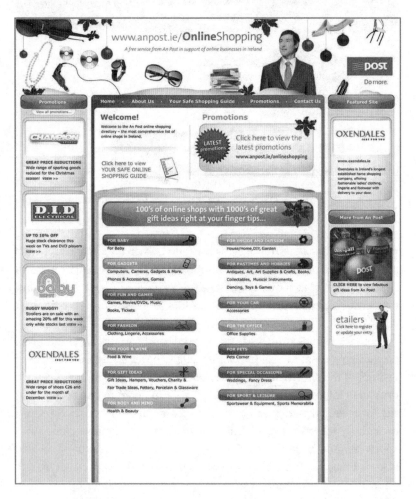

Figure 1.7: An Post.ie / Online Shopping: a product directory

However, over the years, I have seen several directories start and fail because of a flaw at start-up. For suppliers to be willing to pay to advertise, the directory must prove it has good traffic in a specific demographic that will generate leads for the supplier. Launching a web directory can seem something of a chicken and egg situation – how do you get the customers without the suppliers, and how do you get the suppliers without the customers? This conundrum can be rectified easily by offering a six-month period of free advertising for the supplier – creating no barrier to entry for being listed. This fills up the directory, which entices the potential customers seeking a service, which increases hits to the site, and means the directory owner can then re-visit the account with the supplier six months later with significant hits and leads to show them, which then justifies a fee for being listed, or taking a premium listing thereon in.

A sixth business model is a **social portal** – a website that creates a community. An example of this is Facebook (www.facebook.com), which has many, many millions of users.

Closer to home, Friends Reunited (www.friendsreunited.co.uk) was set up in the UK by a couple in 2000. Designed to reunite friends from past schools, colleges or workplaces, the site was an immediate success. Sold to ITV in 2005 for £120m, it was subsequently sold on for a mere £25m, although the site remains active today and has many overseas branches and has further diversified into ancestry searches.

Another example of social portals are the many dating sites now prevalent on the Internet, where users pay a monthly subscription fee to join the site.

Figure 1.8: AnotherFriend.com: a social portal

The social portal is one of the few examples of a business that works in the online environment that wouldn't be nearly as successful offline because of its sheer scalability and reach. In this case, the product offered is 'connection' and sometimes 'introduction to other people'. Traditionally, these sites have worked on an annual subscription fee basis, but of late, with the success of free sites such as Facebook, sites such as Friends Reunited have stopped their annual fees. As with other business models, the primary revenue stream in this instance is from **advertisements** on the site.

Another business model, through usually poor in terms of revenue generation, is a **blog**. A blog is essentially an online diary and personal web page where you can write articles and voice your opinions on current and political issues, the last book you read, or your favourite gadget! Blogs, as with Twitter (a 'micro-blog'), are about having a voice, and creating a following. Many of the most popular blogs in the world are political and technical in their nature.

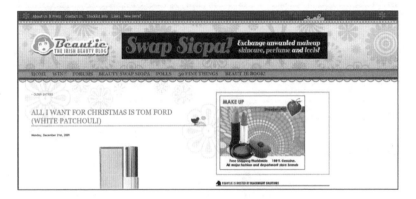

Figure 1.9: Beaut.ie: a blog

There are over 200 million blogs in the world and counting, but the majority have a life span of just three months. A big challenge for bloggers is to continue to produce interesting, new and relevant material on their blog.

> *Blogging is hard because of the grind required to*
> *stay interesting and relevant.*
> **Sufia Tippu**

Business blogging on your chosen profession is becoming increasingly popular. However, recent explosions in the number of blogs on the web means there are now millions of blogs, all clamouring for attention from visitors – as a result, finding a dedicated audience can be difficult. As with the directory of services or information portal model, revenue comes from **advertising**. And to encourage advertisers, you need lots of visitors to your site. Google AdSense is a pay-per-click advertising scheme that any blogger can include on their page, receiving payment only if visitors click on the ads. Perez Hilton (www.perezhilton.com) is one of a rare few successful bloggers, who generate significant advertising revenue from their blogs. Famous for his blogs on celebrity gossip, he now averages over 12 million unique readers a month and his site is littered with high profile television, film and clothing advertising.

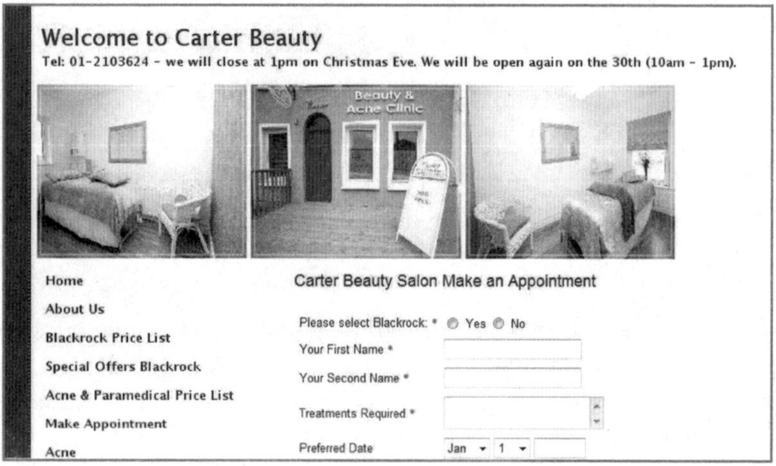

Figure 1.10: Carter Beauty: selling a service online

Selling a service online is yet another Internet business model. A good example of this is a cinema selling tickets to film showings, or a beautician using their website as the first step in the sales process – allowing people to book appointments, while payments are made in person. No shipping is required!

Other models for an Internet business:

- Sports gambling and spread betting.

- Virtual marketplaces that combine product offerings from a variety of shops into one website - www.buy4now.ie is an example of this model.

- Auction sites – **eBay** being the primary example.

- Classified advertising sites, such as Buy & Sell's website.

- Brokerage sites selling, for example, a range of financial products from different vendors – such as insurance, loans, mortgages.

By and large, these sites are launched by existing bricks-and-mortar companies taking their business online.

1.2 INTERNET *VS* BRICKS-AND-MORTAR STORES

Although the Internet is just another marketplace, there are differences between an online shop and a bricks-and-mortar shop, which should be taken into account when considering setting up your own Internet business. There has been a lot of expectation in the past about the great potential of the Internet as a vast marketplace, and a lot of excitement, too. Is it worth all the hype?

When it comes to the list of commonalities that Internet vs bricks-and-mortar stores have in common, there's plenty to include:

- Both Internet and bricks-and-mortar stores are about **footfall** – be it customers visiting the website marketplace, or walking physically into the store. You need customers in your retail space to be able to make money.

- **Customer service** online or off is just as important for both. Online businesses need to provide a good returns policy, and answer customer queries efficiently and effectively on email and telephone. Bricks-and-mortar shops need informed, educated staff and a well-run shop to ensure customers keep coming back for more.

- The basic rules of **pricing** apply to both. Price based on what
  customers are willing to pay, while being aware of your
  competition's price points. Sell off unpopular items at low
  prices to recoup cash to spend on stock that will sell and create
  a profit.

- **Employ marketing** tactics to attract customers – from sales
  and special offers to raising awareness among customers that
  you exist at all.

When it comes to contrasts, the list is not short either:

- Setting up a shop online has a much **lower barrier to entry**
  than bricks-and-mortar businesses. Low financing is required,
  most Internet businesses start out at home in the garage or
  attic, insurance is low, staff requirements are typically low.

- The **potential marketplace** for an online business is many
  times larger than for a bricks-and-mortar shop. Instead of
  having a geographical radius around the shop be your
  potential marketplace, your customers can be anywhere in the
  town, city, country or world. The potential for scaling up your
  operation is much, much greater, and easier, than with actual
  physical shops.

- The flip-side of this is that, for many online shops, **competition
  is much higher** on the Internet than it is on the ground. You
  are not just competing with local shops in your area, or even
  city, but other shops all over the country and world.

> *That's what's great about an Internet business
> – there are very few financial barriers to entry.*
> **Aodhán Cullen, StatCounter.com**

- On top of that, on the Internet the next shop or business is just
  a mouseclick away – making **Internet customers much more
  fickle**. It makes sense that, when the next shop is not a drive

away, but a mere click, customer loyalty is very hard to come by, and similarly it's easy to lose customers to other shops.

- One thing that the Internet model suits very well is **niche businesses** – shops or businesses that would not be able to stay alive from the business they would receive from their geographical locale alone, but when brought online, reach a larger audience and do very well. Examples are hobby businesses like my own – crafts, model-making, knitting or collectibles, such as comics or figurines. For our crafts business, we have customers in the farthest-flung parts of the country, and several of the islands, too. The Internet can make these businesses viable where they never were before.

- A great advantage of Internet-based businesses is the amount of data and **information they can easily collect about their customers**. Information about what they buy, and when, is easily collected online and can be used to provide strongly-targeted marketing programmes, designed to contact customers exactly when they're online, about products they have an interest in. Amazon was the first company to take advantage of this – sending their customers (initially unsolicited) personalised newsletters with suggestions for new books or music based on past purchases. Although this was spam, it was well-received as we all love to hear about a new book or CD that's suitable just for us.

- As well as gathering information about customers, the Internet makes it **easy to communicate with them** on a large scale. Two-way communication happens effortlessly in a bricks-and-mortar store, but usually only on a small scale. With an Internet site, communication can be tailored to the majority of customers who've ever purchased from you, even to individual customers. This may be through newsletters, or a chat forum, or a blog. Two-way feedback is easy to get. I regularly poll my craft supplies chat forum to ask whether people are interested in this product line or that, or to check whether new initiatives are meeting their satisfaction.

- Overall, the **overheads and costs** for an Internet store are usually lower than for a bricks-and-mortar unit. Rents are far lower, insurance costs, staffing levels also, but you do have to spend more on marketing and try a little harder to get your customers and to keep them. That's something we'll be spending more time on later in the book.

So, now that you understand the different business models on the Internet, and can see where your own business might fit, let's look at your business idea more closely.

2

WILL YOUR BUSINESS IDEA WORK ONLINE?

2.1 INTRODUCTION

Before a website is built or a euro changes hands, the first step in setting up your online business is evaluating the suitability of your business idea for the online market. The good news is that, even during this recession of ours, online businesses are doing relatively well.

We're seeing over 100 new online businesses registering each month. In March 2009, we broke a new record for Laser and processed €100m worth of business.
Colm Lyon, CEO, Realex Payments

There is a definite growth in internet businesses because of the relatively low start-up costs and international potential of online businesses.
Eibhlin Curley, Assistant CEO, Dublin City Enterprise Board

However, although the Internet market seems a decent choice for investment during a recession, it is imperative that any business idea is properly researched for suitability for the market it is entering and that risks are carefully measured. That's what we'll be doing next. We're going to look at the suitability of your product for sale in an online environment, the profiles of the customers you seek to attract and their behaviours online and then step through different evaluation stages to see whether your idea has staying power.

2.2 WHAT IS YOUR USP?

How can you know whether your business idea will work on the Internet? The short answer is that there's no way of knowing for sure whether your business will work on the Internet until you try it. But you can start by evaluating your own business idea, if you have one, to see whether it will work well in an online environment.

It is worth remembering that the Internet is simply a marketplace that happens to be based online. Regardless of where the marketplace is based, customers are seeking good quality products, good value for money, and good customer service. The Internet is also a fiercely competitive environment – with other vendors just a mouse click away – and online customers are much more fickle than in the bricks-and-mortar world. A business idea really needs to be sound and well-researched to have a good chance at success online.

In assessing your idea's viability for the online market, the main question you need to ask yourself is whether your idea is unique in some way. This is called your USP – your **unique selling proposition**. The Internet is already somewhat mature, and online merchants and services abound. What does your idea have that no other vendor can offer? Can you offer a unique product or range of products not currently available in your country? While many customers browse globally on the Internet, shipping costs often mean that they ultimately shop locally if they can – presuming that the product quality and price is competitive with any other vendors. Research existing vendors in your country or geographical region. Can you offer better variety / price / faster delivery / ease of shopping that is not currently available and of value to the customer?

When thinking about what makes your idea unique, consider the reasons why customers shop online instead of in bricks-and-mortar shops. Here's a checklist to help:

- **Convenience:** For example, the ability to do major grocery shopping for a small delivery charge. The charge is easily outweighed by the convenience that the service offers, thus making an online sales model viable in this case. It is for convenience that I regularly do my grocery shopping online – the shipping charge is at least half-outweighed by what I would pay in parking charges in most local shopping centres. And having my shopping delivered to my door, rather than spending two tired hours doing it myself, is priceless.

- **Better price:** By shopping online, the customer can get better value – even with a shipping charge included. Amazon.co.uk is a great example of this, eBay also. When purchasing new DVDs for my son, I often buy from CD WOW! – prices are always several euro lower than any shop, and shipping is free.

- **Unique product:** By shopping online, the customer can get products they cannot find or buy in their local stores. Most niche products are good examples here, be they for hobbies, outsize clothing, sports or science fiction. This is also true of brands of clothing, make-up, toys and other items that customers have read about but cannot yet purchase in local stores. My favourite perfume is manufactured in Germany and can't be bought easily in Ireland – so I Googled, and bought it directly from the USA – and for half the price, too. Recently, I bought online for my young son two Enid Blyton *Magic Faraway Tree* books that are out-of-print.

- **Better shopping experience:** The customer may get similar value or choice, and even pay a little extra for shipping the product, but they avoid the hassle of car-parks, traffic or else they are shopping for a hobby or something that they enjoy, and thus enjoy the online shopping experience. Shopping for clothes, music or hobbies are good examples of this.

How can your business offer these factors to customers? And if you can, how can you do it better than your existing, or potential, competitors out there?

For my crafts site, our USP was that we offered a **unique product** you could not find easily in shops in Ireland. Even now, we order from a wide range of suppliers, while most of our competitors choose to source from one main supplier only. We also try to offer a better, and more personal, shopping experience to our customers – providing a forum, classes, and other features that bricks-and-mortar businesses cannot support.

For my wedding site, our USP was **price** and **convenience** – by making it easy for people to make their own wedding stationery, we enable them to save up to 60% of the cost of their invitations. We also offered a unique product – opening up people's choice in their wedding stationery beyond what local shops were providing.

2.3 Does your Product Suit Online Sale?

Consider next the practical suitability of the product you plan to sell through the web. It may be a **physical product** that the customer purchases and has delivered to their door such as clothes, children's toys or food products or it may be a **service** such as a phone subscription, a monthly DVD rental licence, or another non-material item. The same questions apply, regardless of the nature of product you are selling:

- **Does the product display well on screen?** Is an online image of the product enough to convince customers to purchase, or will they need to see it in person? Does the product display well on a 2D monitor? Are true colours required?

- **What is the sales model? Do customers need / want to see the product in person before committing to purchase?** A classic example of this is buying a car. In the USA, most prospective car buyers first research online to find the car they wish to buy, but then visit the dealer's showroom to actually purchase it. A purchase of this size requires a level of emotional investment that makes the product unsuitable for selling solely online.

- **What are the shipping costs?** How high are they? Will they be a barrier to sale for potential customers? In general, customers are willing to pay shipping for items they cannot get locally. For products that can be purchased locally, shipping must not be so high as to encourage the customer to buy offline instead. Consider the size and potential weight of the goods you wish to sell, and research whether a viable, cost-effective shipping method is available.

- **Selling a service through the web:** Selling a service through the web can mean anything from a beautician allowing appointments to be made online, where payment is made in person after the service has been provided in the salon, to an airline selling flight tickets, where the customers pay by credit card and download their own boarding cards. The nature of the service will determine how you model your business on the web. Whether you're enabling the buying or simply booking an appointment online with a restaurant, gardener or solicitor, consider how people go through the sales process with your business and how it fits to the web. It may be enough to allow customers to book an initial free consultation with your practice, or, in some cases, the entire transaction may start and finish with the web.

2.4 WHO ARE YOUR CUSTOMERS?

If you are sure that your idea has 'legs' and that your product can be sold online, the next area to consider is your potential customers:

- What is the demographic for your customer base? Do they purchase online?
- If so, what do they purchase, and when are their peak buying times? In Ireland, many people don't have broadband at home and so they purchase during work hours. In the UK, primary purchase times are centred around weekends.

Do your **market research** on your potential customer base. Statistics are always useful – the number of your target demographic in your chosen catchment area is useful to help you judge potential business for your idea.

Feet-on-the-street research is also imperative. Start by asking family and close friends for their opinions. Then use a survey or other means to get information from a wider group of 30 to 50 friends, associates, and willing participants. Talk to as many potential customers as you can. Ask them whether they would buy your kind of product online. Set up your own online survey using SurveyMonkey.com or PollDaddy.com and ask everyone you know on Facebook or Twitter to take it for you! Use this process to identify any potential pitfalls to the online sales process *before* you take your idea live.

As an example, before launching my Irish crafts supplies site, I did the following:

- **I attended Ireland's largest crafting event and craft supplies show** annually over three years. One year would have been enough – I was attending the other years as a crafter. Each year, there were no Irish paper-crafting providers there. UK and Northern Irish vendors attended the show and sold products at sterling prices, much to the annoyance of the attendees. Nearly all the UK vendors had websites they sold from also.

- I attended a card-making class given by the Crafts Council of Ireland with 40 card makers in attendance. These were 40 potential customers for my craft supplies site and I took the time to speak to as many as possible and asked them all about how they sourced products.

- I researched similar online shops in our closest comparative market – the UK and finding many, counted all I could to get an idea for the relevant market potential in Ireland. I also drew up a database of common products provided by all these sites to give me a good idea of which products to launch my site with.

- I researched statistically as much as I could – finding a lot of information about the crafts markets in the USA and UK (both growing), which then I could compare (to an extent) across to the Irish market, which tends to follow trends in the UK and USA. I found that 20 million people had tried scrapbooking in the previous 10 years – a figure I found encouraging, to say the least.

All this helped me to validate the online card-makers and scrapbooking market, which has subsequently shown itself to be a successful online model.

As an example of one that **didn't work** – I knew that cross-stitching (a form of embroidery) was a hobby with a growing number of fans in Ireland. Though I had not done cross-stitching myself, I decided to start an experimental line of products in the craft. I didn't research it well beforehand, and it utterly failed. The demographic of the fans of the craft was a much older one, not used to purchasing online, and my lack of knowledge of the product meant I did not purchase the right products.

An example of your business idea working well in another market (for example, abroad) is immediate verification for your business idea, though localised tastes and habits must be considered also.

A growing market is always a good place to be. Niche markets work extremely well on the Internet as, by their very nature, customers are often scattered and unable to source the products they need / desire locally. This is an example where the Internet model thrives over and above a local shop, which cannot attract a wide enough audience in its niche to survive.

> *Do it. BUT don't start your own business unless you*
> *have researched your business first.*
> *Research your market and that will tell you whether to*
> *start your own business or not.*
> **Daragh Murphy, HairyBaby.com**

Although reports show a high percentage of small businesses failing in the first year, every entrepreneur I spoke to has no regrets about trying both their successful and unsuccessful ventures.

2.5 KNOW YOUR SALES MODEL

On one of my sites, www.craftsupplies.ie, we have several thousand customers, many of whom return to our site time and time again to place repeat orders. Customers are based all over Ireland, even on the islands, with some in the UK and Europe, and typically they purchase relatively small orders (in the range of €20 to €40) and do so on a regular basis. Orders are usually small and sent by ordinary post. We regularly newsletter our customers, and new products are introduced frequently to encourage repeat business.

On our wedding site, the sales model is quite different. Orders are large, but typically customers will not order more than a handful of times with us – first to purchase wedding stationery, and then to purchase other accessories and details for the day itself. These are typically bulkier purchases and often are sent by courier. There is no ongoing repeat business in general (most people only get married once), and we do not newsletter our customer base often, or worry as much about introducing new products, though on any site new products are needed to maintain continuing interest.

In setting up your own Internet business, it is useful to have an idea as to how it might operate. This enables you to put the correct shipping services in place, to provide good customer service, and to have the right expectations when it comes to the finances of your company. Ask yourself, and more importantly, your potential customers:

- How much do you spend on average on this product?
- How often would you purchase this product?
- Do you use the same sites regularly, or prefer to try new ones?
- How big is my market in Ireland / UK / Europe /the world?

You may be surprised by the answers. In launching a website on the Internet, your business is likely at least to go national immediately – your market, if you are using a .ie domain (more on this later), immediately is all of Ireland, and possibly further, depending on your product's suitability for export. If at all possible, try to find out how many potential customers there are for you in Ireland. Use statistics, or club / group membership numbers if your business is targeted at a specific group, or see how many sites like yours exist abroad, relative to the populations of the country. Use anything you can to get a realistic top-level idea of how big your company can grow to. I've seen many Internet businesses launch with overblown expectations of revenue and sales. At the end of the day, Ireland alone is a very small market of just four million people. In comparison, the UK is nearly 61 million.

So, now you have done the groundwork, it's time to turn to the technicalities of taking your business online.

3
WEBSITE BASICS

3.1 CHOOSING A NAME

If you have evaluated it and found your business idea to be sound, the next thing you need to do is to choose and register your website address, or domain. Here are some tips on choosing a good website name:

- **It needs to be easy to remember:** We are bombarded with so many websites these days, it's impossible to remember them all. While clever names or well-branded names (such as Amazon, Pig's Back) can be cool, they aren't always catchy. A name that relates to the business you do is often the best bet and more likely to be remembered. My crafts supplies site has the website address, www.craftsupplies.ie – it does exactly what it says on the tin.

- **It should be easy to spell:** The Internet is a fickle marketplace, so you don't want customers getting frustrated because you've spelled your site 'kool' instead of 'cool' because, well, you thought it looked cool.

- If you choose **a name that bears no connection to the products or services you sell** (Bebo being an obvious one, Daft.ie is another), be very sure that it's a name that people will remember: By doing this, you are essentially committing yourself to building a new brand for your company / website that people will remember. Check the reactions of family and friends to it before deciding on a final name.

- **If you want Google to find it more easily**, consider using a hyphen if it's a double-word name (for example, www.craft-supplies.ie instead of www.craftsupplies.ie): With a hyphen, Google will recognize the two words separately, and tag the site based on them, rather than tagging "craftsupplies" as a word no one is ever going to type into a search engine. That's the upside of hyphens. The downside is humans in general aren't very fond of them – they seem a little 'messy', and harder to remember.

At the end of the day, the decision is yours, and you will likely be influenced by sites you know already that you think are good. In choosing the names of my do-it-yourself wedding stationery sites, I chose DIYWedding, www.diywedding.ie. At the same time, I also registered www.diyweddings.ie and forwarded the name to our site in case anyone remembered it slightly wrong. It's worked well for us. It's very easy to remember, and purposely left us open to grow beyond stationery – which we have done – to include DIY favours, car ribbon, table decorations, pew bows … the list goes on.

For all of my sites, I have also purchased names that are similar to my own websites, which may be mistyped by people into browsers – for example, www.diyweddings.ie or www.caracraftsupplies.ie instead of www.craftsupplies.ie. It doesn't cost much to purchase the extra domains, and then most domain registries allow you to 'forward' the domain to another URL – so if you type in www.diyweddings.ie, it automatically forwards you to www.diywedding.ie, invisibly to the person typing. Web-forwarding like this can help you to capture traffic that you might otherwise miss.

3.2 REGISTERING YOUR DOMAIN

Once you've chosen your website name, the next step is to see if it's available or has been taken already. An easy way to do this is to navigate either to www.whoislookup.ie (for Irish domain names) or www.whois.net (for most other domain names). If the name you're looking for is still free, great – go ahead and register it! If not, try again.

.ie or .com?
When choosing a domain name, you need to decide whether to choose a **.ie** address, **.com** or both. How can you decide? What should influence your decision?

- If all, or even the majority of, your customers are expected to be **based in Ireland**, a **.ie** is best. It is an immediate signal to customers that you are based in Ireland. Nearly all customers prefer a local vendor – it bodes better where shipping costs and customer services are concerned.

- If you plan to run an internationally-traded business with **customers based abroad**, it may be better to choose **.com**. The problem with this is that virtually all usable .com addresses have already been taken, so you will be forced to choose an over-long or hard-to-remember name. You'll need to be inventive to come up with a catchy name that's still available. Also, some people assume that .com means you are based in the USA.

- What about **.eu** addresses? Some time ago, .eu addresses were opened up to the public, and many Irish people purchased them. For European-traded businesses, this is a solution with potential, but the reality is they are not in widespread use yet. However, as .coms become more and more unavailable though, this may change.

If you Google "register .ie domain" or similar words on Google.ie, a host of companies offering the service will come up. At the time of

going to press, Let's Host (www.letshost.ie) was providing the best deal, with registration being offered for just €17.99 for a .ie domain. Black Knight (www.blacknight.com) is never far behind and also offers good deals for domain registration. Other sites such as www.register.ie will charge up to €69.99 – so it's worth shopping around.

Requirements for registering a .ie website address

When you are registering a .ie website, the IEDR (IE Domain Registry) will check what entitlement you have to the address – what right you have to own it. If you are building a site for a business, you will need either a Registered Business Name, or to be a Limited Company – visit the Companies Registration Office (www.cro.ie) for information on both. Trademarks and personal names are also accepted (if the site name matches them). To see the exact policies, visit the IEDR's website at www.iedr.ie.

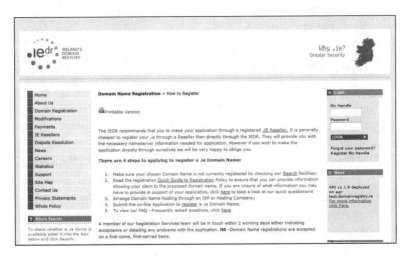

Figure 3.1: IEDR / domainregistry.ie

The registration process only takes a week or two if you have your business name and number already. Once you have received confirmation of your registration, you are allowed to add content to your website address, and go live.

3.3 CHOOSING AN INTERNET HOST PROVIDER

Registering your domain name gives you the right to own that website name, but it doesn't automatically buy a place for the website to 'live' and store its data. The next step after registration (sometimes done during registration) is to choose an Internet Host Provider (IHP) to **host** your website. An IHP provides website owners with access to computers on which you store your website information. These computers (called 'servers', since they 'serve' information), are always on, and are much more powerful than your home computer. You store your website content on them, so that should anyone want to visit your website at any time, the server ensures your website is viewable at all times. In theory, you could use your home computer as a host provider – store all your pages on it and keep it permanently on – but it would be more expensive than using an IHP and also wouldn't handle high-volume periods or sudden peaks in demand very well.

There was a time when host provider packages in the USA were superior to those offered at home in Ireland, but Irish host providers have caught up and there is little to choose between the offerings at home and abroad.

One reason to host in a particular country is if your customers reside there. Google takes notice of where your site is hosted when it does its rankings for different countries, so if you are hosted in Ireland, you have a higher chance of being ranked better on Google.ie / Google Ireland searches, which is what you want. If, on the other hand, your customers reside abroad, it's worthwhile considering hosting there. For example, Aodhán Cullen of StatCounter.com has two million users of his web statistics software worldwide. Over 40% are based in the US (Ireland barely even figures in his top countries), so he hosts in the USA, too.

The key things to consider when choosing an IHP are:

- Support.
- Spam.
- Features.
- Statistics.

First, what is their support package like? Is it 24 hours? Is it phone and email? If you are running an online business such as a shop, you need to make sure support is there whenever you need it so you don't lose business. If you are running a marketing website for your company, outage is not as distressing, though certainly not desirable. Be sure to ask for the support terms before signing up.

Does the IHP have a policy for filtering out email spam? Most do, but some don't.

What web features does the IHP support? Which packages have databases, scripting support, is it Windows-based or Linux-based? Most marketing sites need very little features and can use the entry level packages from an IHP, but if you want a newsletter box on your front page for people to sign up, you may need scripting features and database support. Talk to your developer before signing up with a plan.

The wonderful thing about websites is how measurable they are – and a lot of this information can come from your IHP statistics package. Ask them for information about the statistics packages they provide. Think about what you will want.

The kind of information I regularly check for my sites includes:

- **Number of visits per week / month:** This shows how many visits there have been to your site. You may have heard of statistics on the number of **hits** being bandied around, but this is an inaccurate estimate to use. Each item downloaded constitutes a 'hit' – a picture or a frame (section of a web page) – so for one page, you might get 10 or 20 hits, but only one person visiting it.

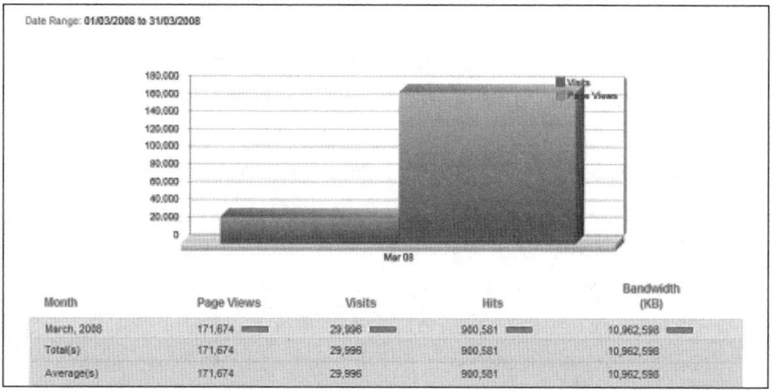

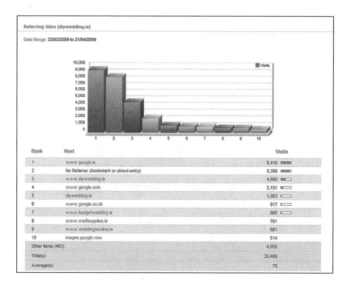

Figure 3.2: Site statistics – visitor numbers

- **Referring sites:** This tells you how visitors found your site – via Google, via a directory you may have advertised with, via a mention you got on a forum – and is a vital measurement for your marketing data.

Figure 3.3: Site statistics – referring sites

- **Top search phrases / keywords:** If people found you through Google, what did they search for? This statistic shows the popularity of various search terms – for example, do people searching for "books" tend to buy more from you than those searching for "dvds". This information enables you to hone your marketing to make it as cost-effective as possible and to generate the most actual sales.

- **Search engine visits:** Google and other search engines have software programs referred to as 'bots' or 'spiders' that constantly search the web, going from website to website, cataloguing and categorising each one. While you don't have control over them, it's useful to know when they've been and whether your site is getting attention from them or not.

- **Top pages:** See the pages that are most often viewed by visitors. Your home page will usually be first, and from there you can see which information is of most importance to your visitors.

- **Daily totals:** See summaries of all visits by days. This is useful to see when your site is most visited. For example, on our Irish DIYWedding.ie site, the vast majority of the shopping / browsing is done on weekdays but, in the UK, it all happens at the weekend. This gives you useful information to determine, for example, when the best time to send a newsletter to your customers might be.

Other information that may be of interest includes:

- The **browser and platform** visitors are using: If a lot of your visitors are using Mozilla Firefox (a lesser known alternative to Microsoft's Internet Explorer, that now has nearly 20% of the market), for example, you can make sure your site is tested on all platforms / browsers being used by visitors.

- The **top downloads** people are taking from your site: If you have a number of information sheets, a brochure, etc., you can see what people are choosing to download.

- **The entry and exit pages** through the site: See where people enter your site, and more importantly, where they exit from, to learn more about how successful your site is in capturing the leads you want.

If you are not offered this kind of data by your IHP, the free (Irish) statistics product StatCounter (www.statcounter.com) is an excellent alternative. You need to add some code to your site to allow it to measure visitor information for you, but it provides free hosting for the statistics information and package and is extremely popular worldwide.

There are many different companies offering host services in Ireland, with more entering the market all the time – for example, companies like HostingIreland.ie, LetsHost.ie, Blacknight.com (these guys come with a good reputation), IrishHosting.net and WebWorld.ie. When I first started out, I asked for recommendations from friends in the software industry, got a good one, and went with that. It's done me no harm and I've used them for every subsequent site since. Ask around, use your checklist, and take it from there.

4
BUILDING A MARKETING BROCHURE WEBSITE

4.1 INTRODUCTION

Probably the biggest challenge to overcome, particularly for those with a business idea but little technical knowledge, is getting your website built and off the ground. Boutique website houses will quote scary figures, upwards of €5,000, and even €10,000. How do you know whether you really need such an expensive site? Are there other options out there? How much is the whole thing going to cost? These, and lots of other questions, are the focus for this chapter.

There are several options available for building a website:

- Build the website yourself from scratch.

- Purchase a reusable template off the shelf and pay a lower cost to have it tailored and integrated.

- Build your website using a basic website builder – software provided free on the Internet or from your host provider.

- Find a student / brother / friend with IT knowledge to develop your site for you.

- Hire a professional, local development house to build the site for you.

- Hire an overseas website development house – in India, Russia or Poland, for example.

Before we go further, you need to know that there are two main components to a website:

- The **'front end'**: This is the look and feel – colours, fonts, graphics, etc – of your website. The skills required to do this are usually creative and mostly done separately to the back end, though some standalone developers can do both.

- The **'back end'**: This is the shop software that slots in behind the elegant front end and provides you with the invoicing, product management, order management, etc. This software usually sits on top of a database – which is like a large filing cabinet that stores all your information about your customers, orders, products – and the shop software pulls the information out as it is requested and needed by you.

So who does what, in the different build options above?

- If you build the website yourself, you will need to build both the front and back ends;

- If you use a template – the template, once modified by you, **is** the front end – it is the look and feel of your site, and then you integrate it with the back end shop software;

- If you use a site-builder, you will build a very basic front end yourself, which is typically used as a basic brochure site;

- If you use a friend / family member to build your website, check that they can do both for you;

- If you use a local software house, they will nearly always build both for you and include them in the price;

- If you use an overseas house, they will do both for you typically.

Because the work involved in building an online shop site is so much greater than that involved in building what I call a 'marketing brochure' site, I am going to split my advice about building websites into two separate sections. For this chapter, we'll delve into what is by far the more common site that business owners build – a marketing brochure website.

This type of site outlines what your company does, what is unique about you and why customers would want to do business with you, and provides contact information or a form to enable customers to take the next step to doing business with you. These sites apply to every business out there and are a truly great way of getting the word out easily and to a very wide audience.

4.2 MY EXPERIENCE OF BUILDING WEBSITES

I'm lucky to have a Computer Science background and was able to build them myself, though I had never built a site in my life before I built mine. It has saved me a lot of money and meant I could bring my websites to market very quickly after the ideas were thought up and researched. I have three online shop sites and one 'brochure' site, containing just information (www.budgetwedding.ie).

For the shop sites, I purchased very cheap shop software (just $50 at the time), which gave me all I needed to create an online shop quickly, with product descriptions, optional extras, a category set-up for browsing the site, invoicing and stock management and a database behind it all to hold all the product information. The software I used was called Candypress (www.candypress.com) and is designed for use in a Windows ASP hosting environment. It provided back end shop, stock and invoicing software, and a basic front end that I tweaked to match our colour scheme and have our logo.

Initially, I had chosen OSCommerce – free open-source software – but, at the time, it ran much better on Linux / Unix than it did on Windows. I had already chosen my hosting package, and after a week of trying to get OSCommerce working in that environment, I gave up and switched to Candypress. I have heard nothing but good things about OSCommerce though, and another product like it – ZenCart, which is a PHP version of OSCommerce. But, at the time, I was in a great rush to bring my site live, and that definitely played a part in my choice of Candypress, as I had it up and running in hours.

A good number of Irish Internet businesses opt to use custom-built software for online shops built by Irish web development houses. Usually this is licensed on an annual basis, and comes with good support features. It's a more expensive option, but a good one for those who like the feeling of a proper support system close at hand. Things can, and do, go wrong with online shopping software, and I've had more than one panic-filled day because of it. From people I spoke to for the case studies in this book, they were very happy with the set-up they had chosen.

4.3 BUILD THE WEBSITE YOURSELF

For many people, the question 'Is building my website myself an option?' is a 'Yes' or 'No' question. The question could be re-phrased as 'Do you have web development skills?'. If your answer is 'Yes', build the website yourself; if your answer is 'No', hire someone else to do it.

Building your own site from scratch requires at least basic web development skills and computer experience. Creating a simple marketing brochure site requires some knowledge of web technologies like html and, in some cases, XML, XSL or PHP or other scripting languages. Nonetheless, a website that simply has content and pictures can be easier to create than you might think. Some host providers provide their own site wizards, or free ones are available too Depending on the sophistication of each, some can enable you to build a relatively professional-looking website.

If you go ahead with building your own website, you'll need a good HTML editor (see **Chapter 9: Resources**, for a summary of web development languages and terms). The best-known editors are:

- **Kompozer's** big advantage is that it's free, but it can be hard to figure out how to do some of the most basic edits with this freeware.

- **Microsoft's Sharepoint Designer** was made free in April 2009. The successor to MS Frontpage, Sharepoint is an adequate editor that does most of what the average website builder requires. Custom extensions have long since disappeared from the product, meaning websites built using it will work on any platform.

- **Macromedia's Dreamweaver** has long been the holy grail of web editors. It takes a little time to learn – a tutorial or some instruction from a friend is advised – but, once you're on your way, it offers great flexibility and features to make a truly great website. It's expensive, though – several hundred euro for the most basic version.

Some of the Enterprise Centres and Enterprise Boards offer reasonably-priced courses on basic web design. Check your local Enterprise Centre / Board for information – go to www.enterpriseboards.ie.

The decision to build your own site is a personal one. If you have a technical leaning and can learn quickly and well on your own, or through a training course, you may enjoy building and getting your website off the ground. If it's not something that appeals, I'd recommend not even trying. There are a lot of finicky bits involved in building a website – patience is required, and you may just end up tearing your hair out instead. If you are committed to the idea, the website http://build-website.com gives a good overview on the background, tools and steps required to build your own website. A million others exist – just type 'build your own website' into Google.

4.4 USE A TEMPLATE

The next option is a little like number 1, the build-it-yourself option, but with less effort. I tried this option recently with my www.budgetwedding.ie site. I purchased a website template for $50 from www.templatemonster.com – but only after I had researched www.websitetemplates.com and several other sites, too. There are free website templates available also, but I found they invariably looked less professional than the ones with a small price tag to their name.

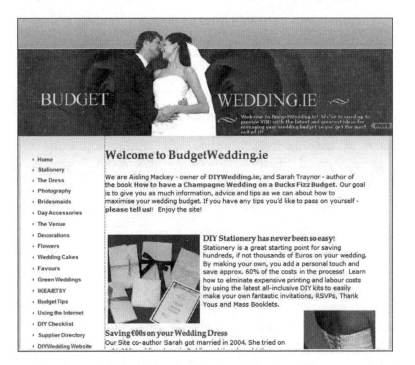

Figure 4.1: BudgetWedding.ie – built using a template

I then spent a day or two familiarising myself with Adobe Photoshop (a graphic editing programme), to tailor the template to include my titles and, in some places, images, and thus saved the several hundred euro it would have cost to have this work done for me. All I had to do was minor edits and add content, and the site was ready in days.

This works well if you have some technical knowledge, as many people do, but don't have all the skills needed to create a professional-looking graphically-designed site.

TIP: Another option is to merge two of the approaches and **buy the template** and save €€€ on the costs of graphically designing the site, then **pay a developer** to integrate it with your shopping cart back end software. Doing this can save you thousands of euro.

The downside of using a template? Unless you're willing to pay several hundred dollars for the template, it won't be unique. Many will have been downloaded several times already. This means there is the remote possibility that someone else will have a site that looks like yours, but the reality is that most of the downloads are in the USA and are unlikely to be used by someone with a similar business close to you. Also, if you are concerned about it, it's not difficult to change the colour of a background or the font of a title and create a unique look for your site. And the chances are that everyone else who downloaded the template is doing the same!

4.5 USE A WEBSITE-BUILDER

If you're a beginner or just starting out with a very basic website, website-builder tools are worth trying out. These are easy-to-use tools that allow you to create and edit a basic website, usually from a template, and are offered by some IHPs. There are also several free on the Internet.

In addition, Yahoo, Microsoft and other companies offer free web pages and a site-builder to create a basic website, but most of these will be hosted by them on their own URLs – for example: Google's 'easy-to-use' site-builder tool can be found at https://sites.google.com/. It provides a limited number of business / professional templates, since it is more targeted at personal websites and clubs / groups. Sites set up using the builder have the url https://sites.google.com/sitename/, so it is immediately obvious that the site is hosted by Google and is not a full professional site.

> *I used a basic and easy website builder and built my first*
> *website myself – but it was very basic.*
> **Maebh Collins, TheNaturalBabyResource.com**

Irish site-builders that look appealing, such as http://www.myweb.ie, usually aren't suitable for more established businesses as they provide a limited number of templates for the websites, so duplication is probable, and they are typically more targeted at personal rather than business sites.

Irish host providers Blacknight.com, IrishDomains.com, DarkLite.ie and LetsHost.ie all provide their own site-builder tools. Some look better than others; http://www.simplehosting.ie has a large range of basic templates and offers a good deal.

I built my first, incredibly basic, site using Yahoo's Geocities website-builder – now available at http://sitebuilder.yahoo.com. It was fine, but basic, as many of them are.

4.6 USE A FRIEND / RELATIVE WITH IT KNOWLEDGE

The fourth option when creating your website is to find a friend, relative or someone you know who has a technical background and training, and is interested in earning some money on the side and can create a website for you. This is a really good option if you know someone who's done good work and wants the job.

The plusses are a lower-priced website for you, together with someone who is local and who will understand your requirements well, and can offer some support once the site goes live. The downside is that projects like these often go well over deadlines and it can be hard to get your site up and running in the timeframe that you'd like. The nature of the agreement is usually that the developer in question is either a student or someone working in the computer industry, and thus will be creating your site in his / her spare time. If this suits you, then by all means go for it – I'd recommend it. But if you are launching a business within a specific timeframe, you're probably better off choosing one of the other options.

4.7 HIRE A LOCAL DEVELOPMENT HOUSE

Option five – to hire a professional Irish website development company to build your site – is at the other end of the costs scale from building it yourself.

As with all things in life, when it comes to websites, it is true that you get what you pay for. If you're looking for a truly slick, modern, dynamic website, then consider using one of the many domestic professional website houses in Ireland.

To give you an idea of prices, I submitted requests for quotes to several leading Irish website houses for a website with the following specification, typical of many marketing brochure sites:

- Basic marketing brochure website;

- Approximately 10 to 20 static pages (no Flash or dynamic HTML);
- 10 images or so;
- A 'Contact Us' form;
- A 'Sign up to Our Newsletter' form;
- A wedding website theme.

The resulting quotes started at €800 and went up as high as €3,000 for a high-end, upmarket site. The average quote was between €1,200 and €1,500.

A great advantage of dealing with an Irish website design company is that you have great flexibility with your design, lots of opportunities to evolve your website as it is built, and a local support number to call if you have any problems once it's launched. This is not to be underestimated. My sites have gone down more than once – two of them have been hacked. I have developers that I use to work on them when I cannot, but there is total panic when a site **does** go down. Knowing you have a local company you can call on in such cases is a great advantage indeed.

When using an Irish website design company, you don't need any technical knowledge as such (though it's always good to have someone with some technical background to review your plans and the site as it progresses). You do need to know what you want from your site, what kind of image you wish to project, what content you want on the site, and ideally, the general look and feel you'd like for your site. Have a look at competitors' websites or other sites you like the look and feel of. The closer you can describe what you need, the better the chance you have of it being delivered to you.

Do check for post-development support, and enquire how further updates can be made to the site once it is finished. Apply for several quotes and find a company you feel you can work well with.

4.8 HIRE AN OVERSEAS WEBSITE DEVELOPMENT HOUSE

If you don't have a large budget, or strong technical knowledge, it's worth considering having your website built offshore for you, using one of the many burgeoning website development companies in countries like India, Russia and Poland.

The major advantage of using an offshore company is that it's cheap. The most it's likely to cost is a couple of hundred euro, so it's worth trying almost from that perspective alone.

I have used www.rentacoder.com a lot over the past five years for one-off design work and brochure-type websites. I would pay one-10th of what I would pay for an Irish-based development company and it would be completed in one-10th of the time … however, I would say that, if you use these services, you need to be very detailed in your requirements and know what you are talking about. If you need someone to hand-hold you through developing a website, this route would not be for you and I would go with an Irish company instead.

Web developer

The major disadvantage is that it's a very restrictive development process, no hand-holding is provided, so you need to have an extremely clear plan for what you wish to achieve from your website, and this takes time in advance planning. You may also have to spend time after the site is delivered fixing errors.

The typical development process with an overseas development house is:

- On signing up, typically you will be asked to **fill out a questionnaire** saying what content you want for your site, how many pages, how many images, how many forms (if any) and to provide several existing websites of a similar look and feel or genre to allow the developers to use them as a guide for what you want. This is essentially a requirements / design specification for the foreign developer and needs to be quite detailed. It can take some time to put together.

- The website development company will respond with **several sample websites** for look and feel.

- **You choose your favourite website, and suggest any changes** you'd like made. Once agreed, the website content is developed and delivered to you, usually within a couple of weeks.

Problems like unrealistic delivery estimates and communication difficulties can happen, and once the site is handed over, that's it – there is no further support offered typically. If the site you're building is a simple brochure-style site, and you don't expect it to be your primary source of sales, this option is worth looking into. If not, it may be worth considering some of the other options.

Other sites like www.nixers.com and www.freelancer.com also provide the same kind of service to help you to find foreign developers looking for work. As with the build-it-yourself option, the most popular choice for shopping cart software for this option is Open Source cart software.

So there are several options, some of which can be combined. Which you choose depends on your skills, your needs – and your budget! **Table 4.1** on the next page will help you recap the differences.

Table 4.1: Website build options

Build option	Website design knowledge required?	Cost?	Flexibility / ability to change?	Keep to deadline?	Professional look / feel
Build it yourself	Yes	Very low	High	Depends	Medium
Purchase re-usable template	Yes	Low	Medium	Depends	Medium
Use basic free sitebuilder	A little	Low	Low	Depends	Low
Use friend / relative	No	Low	Medium	Not usually good	Low
Hire local web development house	No	High	High	Very good	High
Hire overseas web development house	Some knowledge recommended	Low	Low	Good	Medium

5

BUILDING A SHOP ONLINE

5.1 CHOOSING SHOPPING CART SOFTWARE

When going beyond a marketing brochure website to set up an actual shop online, several additional features are needed, and the project involved to build the website becomes much more complex. For starters, the following need to be considered:

- The site will need to support **secure online payments**.
- The shop will need to have a **database** to contain the products being sold.
- **Statistical information** should be accessible to enable you to track customer trends, marketing projects, product popularity, seasonal trends and many other pieces of data.
- **Stock inventory** needs to be managed.
- **Invoicing** for customers needs to be supported.
- **Shipping costs and methods** need to be factored in, based on what the customer purchases and where they live.
- The ability to capture contact details so you can send **newsletters** to your customers should be provided.
- Products need to be **photographed** and displayed clearly for online viewing.

The list goes on ... The great news is that there's lots of software out there today that can manage all of these features for your online shop. And the best news of all? Many of the software packages are free.

5.2 CHOOSING SHOPPING CART SOFTWARE WHEN BUILDING YOURSELF

When building your online shop yourself, or using a friend or relative to do it for you, the most popular option for shopping cart software is Open Source free cart software such as OSCommerce, ZenCart, CubeCart or a whole host of other programmes. The most popular choices are OSCommerce and ZenCart, its PHP-based successor. The main differences between the two are in the underlying architecture of their code and design. Both have a very complete set of features, and a module to sell downloads (.pdfs, software) is included as well.

Open Source software means that the software is not built by a commercial company but rather by a collection of individuals who create the code voluntarily and for free. The Open Source movement is a large and growing group committed to providing and maintaining software applications available to the public free of charge. The great advantage of these systems, particularly as they are quite mature and well-tested at this stage, is that they're highly functional and full of features and, of course, they are free. The downside is that you don't get support in the bundle with them – if something goes wrong, as it sometimes will, you have to scour the message boards that are used to support the software. I have had to do this many times, but now I have a developer in the UK whom I use on a regular basis to do work on my site. Like many web developers, he always works remotely and I have yet to meet him face-to-face!

There are so many fully-functional shopping cart applications out there that it really comes down to a personal decision as to which you prefer. Or simply go with the most popular, as they are likely to have the most extra features and the best support. If you'd like to investigate further, check out this Wikipedia table, which compares a huge number of shopping carts against a pretty standard list of features: http://en.wikipedia.org/wiki/Comparison_of_shopping_cart_software.

5.3 Shopping Cart Software Provided by a Web Development House

If you use a local software development house to build your site, many provide their own shopping cart software, which they use to develop your site. From the new businesses I've talked to, this is often feature-complete, comprehensive and easy-to-use. The software usually includes management of the product database, invoicing, stock control and even statistics. Pricing usually is on an annual license fee basis – anything in the region of €1,000 to €5,000 annually. Check out the price in advance so you know what to expect, but so far I've received pretty positive responses on this particular cart software option.

5.4 Taking Payment Online

Setting up shop online means being able to take Laser or credit card payments securely through your website. We'll break this into three sections:

- Sorting out a merchant account with your bank (this doesn't apply if you use eBay as your storefront, or WorldPay / PayPal as your payment processor but does for most payment providers).
- Choosing a credit / debit card processor (*aka* online payment processor).
- Deciding whether to host secure payments yourself or use someone else's secure payment server.

Getting a merchant account

A merchant account is an agreement with your bank that enables you to accept credit and debit card payments. Taking credit card payments means there is a fraud risk associated with your bank account, and so the banks require your business bank accounts to be in good order and able to handle frauds, should they occur. There is also a contingent liability – the situation where, for whatever reason, a business may be required to refund against a large number of completed transactions.

One of the first decisions you have to make is whether to apply for a merchant account with your bank and use an online payment processor, such as Realex, to manage your debit and credit cards via your bank (AIB and Bank of Ireland use Realex for their online payment processing). The big advantage of doing this is that you get much more reasonable rates. The disadvantage is that you have to pay both bank charges and fees to the online payment processor.

Chapter 9: Resources provides a sample checklist of what is required to apply for a merchant account with your bank. If you have any previous history of trading, or financial support, this can work in your favour when applying. The requirements for your website don't always have to be fully in place – for example, it's hard to put a secure payment system in place when you don't have the merchant account details to give to the payment service providers, who then won't sign you up! Essentially the banks are looking for businesses that are trading fairly online and properly supporting customer rights.

Trading online without a merchant account

You don't need a merchant account to trade online. Several companies will provide you with payment gateway services, instead of a merchant account – for example, PayPal, WorldPay and Authorize.net. The downside of these services typically is higher transaction fees, but they do enable you to start trading before you have a merchant account and enable you to build up a trading history to help you apply for a merchant account at a later date should you wish to.

I use merchant gateways for all my sites but, in the past, I have used PayPal to process debit card transactions. The good news is that setting up your site to use PayPal and similar options is very easy, and most people are familiar with using it, thanks to the prolific nature of eBay. An account is not required for people to pay through it either, which is worth pointing out to your customers.

Shopping cart software typically is responsible for managing the stock inventory, customer management and invoicing for your online shop. The software may take credit card details or you may redirect customers to a secure payment gateway instead. Typically, shopping carts act as a front end that passes information via a secure connection (another service) to a payment gateway – a separate service altogether.

Choosing a payment provider

Table 5.1 on the next page shows some of the leading payment providers commonly used by online businesses in Ireland (*all information correct at time of going to press*).

PayPal and 2Checkout are both options that don't require a merchant account to be set up in advance but have very high per-transaction rates and, at times, unusual policies for clearing funds into your account – funds can be delayed coming through these payment providers where, with others, it is pretty much instant.

Realex, DataCash and WorldNet all offer similar services with varying price packages and models. WorldNet and Realex were set up by Irish businesses, which can often offer better, local support and services, while DataCash is based out of the UK but services European and even worldwide.

Examine your predicted transaction levels, and telephone all the different providers! Check that they can process Laser cards, as well as the usual credit cards (Visa, Mastercard). See who offers the best deal – the sign-up deals are changing all the time in a very competitive marketplace. Pick the one that best suits you and your business model.

Table 5.1: Online payment providers

	Payment Fee Structure	Merchant Account Required?
2Checkout	5.5% commission on each transaction, plus a $0.45 charge per transaction.	No
DataCash	£960 annual fee. £100 per month. £100 per 1,000 authorisation requests. Enquire for higher transaction level rates.	Yes
PayPal	3.4% + €0.35 transaction fee starting out. Low of 1.9% for €100K per month through PayPal.	No
Realex	Monthly fee €29 – includes 350 free transactions. Additional transactions charged at €0.19 each. 3Dsecure transactions free.	Yes
WorldNet	€30 per month. €0.25 per transaction.	Yes
WorldPay	Monthly fee: GBP 30.00 Transaction fee: 4.5% on the value of credit and non-UK debit card transactions. Set-up fee: GBP 200.00.	Yes

Note that the transaction fees listed above are **only for the online payment processing** – you will also pay the normal fees to your bank for processing credit and debit cards through them.

Securing payments

If you want to provide a 'secure' payments gateway for your website, you have two options:

- **Option 1: Host the payments yourself:** When you purchase a product online, typically you click on the shopping cart, and the 'Checkout' button. You then enter your shipping details and arrive at the payment page. At this point, you may still be on the shop's website itself – if it is hosting the payment transaction themselves, you should see a 'padlock' symbol appear at the bottom of your browser screen. Then you submit your credit card details securely. If the company allows you to store your details for next time, it makes for ease of shopping next time around. If the company is hosting payments itself, it means it is responsible for the secure transmission and (where chosen) storage of your credit card details to the bank's server in order to process the transaction. If the company chooses to allow customers store their credit details, the company is responsible for making sure that no one can hack in to the database that stores sensitive credit card information, or the connection over which the credit card information is sent. This is a big responsibility and requires a lot of software, hardware and expertise.

- **Option 2: Use a payment provider:** In the second option, you go through the payment process just as you did in the previous one, but without noticing (typically) the payment page changing URL over to a payment provider's server instead.

I chose this latter option – to re-direct payments through a payment provider for my sites as it is much easier and also because the responsibility for security thus lies with them. For something so sensitive, I'd rather leave it to the experts, and experts they are.

While there are many different payment providers out there, as shown in the earlier table, the company I use is Realex, www.realexpayments.com, and I've found them to be excellent. I had to integrate my shopping cart with their payment gateway myself, but their support was, and always has been, excellent. I'm a fan of the company – they contacted me a year into my contract with them, and again recently, to lower my per-transaction rates based on my volumes – I've yet to have any other supplier offer to do the same thing.

The only real downside of re-directing your payments is that you cannot store credit card information yourself, so if a payment goes wrong, the credit card details need to be provided by the customer again and, if a customer returns, they will need to enter their details again also.

For more information on taking payments on your website, see a new and useful website, **www.webpayments.ie**.

Website security

During my years in software, I spent some time working as a security consultant for a well-known software company. I learned a lot about various encryption and authorisation methods and where the vulnerabilities lie. While SSL (Secure Sockets Layer) is used to encrypt most online transactions, the reality is it would take a very large computer to break the encrypted connection between your computer and the online shop you are visiting. And all that would be gained would be a single credit card number. It would be easier to steal the credit card directly from a wallet and much less expensive. The true vulnerabilities lie in where the credit cards are stored. Like the gang who stole 40 million credit cards from TK Maxx's databases in the USA, hackers are much more likely to go after larger wins such as the databases storing thousands, if not millions, of your customers' credit card details. While storing credit cards makes transactions a little easier for the customer, in reality it is one of the most vulnerable parts of doing business on the web.

5.5 USING EBAY OR AMAZON AS YOUR SHOPFRONT

An alternative to setting up a full shop online is to sell goods through a widely-established storefront, such as Amazon or eBay. Both of these behemoths now allow you to set up a storefront to sell through their store. This is a low cost way of starting to sell, and a useful way to test the market with products you are considering selling in a full online store without investing heavily in marketing or website costs.

In both cases, the sites charge a monthly fee – starting at just $15.99 for eBay, and $59.99 for Amazon. Amazon also charges a 7% per transaction fee, and eBay requires payment through PayPal – which is expensive and, as it happens, a wholly-owned subsidiary of eBay.

While eBay's fees are lower, it is known primarily as an auction site, though you can purchase items on a 'buy it now' basis and complete the transaction immediately. It tends to be used for people looking for bargains or items they can't find through standard shops. This perhaps explains, in part at least, why their fees are much lower than Amazon's. Anyone with a credit card and a verified PayPal account can set up an eBay storefront.

Amazon, on the other hand, offers a huge audience ready to shop and, while they still maintain a warehouse and sell products directly themselves, they have been moving more and more over to their network of approved sellers in recent years.

You can have an eBay or Amazon store and your own online shop as well – but cross-marketing to your own store from either Amazon or eBay is not permitted – you are not even allowed to mention the name, URL or contact details of any kind of your online store on your eBay or Amazon store. Amazon and eBay want the business to go through their site, not yours.

The advantages of selling solely through Amazon or eBay as your storefront include:

- You don't need to build your own online shop – you can use Amazon / eBay's tools to build one through their site, much more quickly and without expense.
- Immediate access to the Amazon / eBay shopping audience.
- Just your existence on either of these sites means a lot of marketing is automatically done for you.

However, the disadvantages of selling through Amazon / eBay include:

- You only have access to Amazon / eBay customers.

- Monthly and per transaction fees for both.
- On eBay, products must be re-listed every time they are sold, though templates can be used.
- All transactions are subject to customer reviews (this can put pressure on you when you are starting out).
- On eBay, people go to it expecting the best deals and prices on the market – so to compete, you have to offer this as well.

Overall, Amazon / eBay are good places to start out and test the market for your business idea.

5.6 OTHER COSTS INVOLVED IN SETTING UP A SHOP ONLINE

As mentioned by more than one of the case studies in the book (see **Chapter 8**), the good news is that when setting up online, the costs are usually relatively low compared to bricks-and-mortar businesses, but you still need to factor them in when planning. The costs of an online start-up include:

- **Stock:** How much stock you start with is entirely up to you and depends on the product you intend to sell. From our case studies, Maebh from **TheNaturalBabyResource.com** started with just €100. I started with €5,000, and others started with less than this. Most online businesses grow organically – test the product in the market, see how it does. Sell one, buy two more; sell two, buy four more and so on.
- **Premises:** Every entrepreneur I spoke to started out in a shed, a spare room or a garage – and graduated from there. Talk to your parents, dust out your attic, empty out the spare room. If you absolutely require professional premises, contact your local Enterprise Board (**www.enterpriseboards.ie**) for a list of Enterprise Centres and workspaces in your area – these will

often offer smaller incubation spaces with general office facilities and meeting rooms at hand more so than other business buildings. Enterprise Centres also offer month-to-month rolling contracts so you can grow into larger units as you need to, without being confined to a long-term restrictive lease. I started in an aunt's attic, before moving to a tiny commercial premises, approx. 100 sq ft in size, in which we lasted six months. Then we were lucky enough to apply to Terenure Enterprise Centre and got a larger space there, then a larger one again within the centre a year later, and then into our current premises near Sandyford.

- **Registering your company:** This is usually done by your accountant with the CRO and costs a couple of hundred euro. It's one of the first things you should do when setting up your business.

- **Company insurance:** This shouldn't be much to start with and usually includes stock value, public liability, employers' liability and material damage if you are manufacturing. Premiums usually can be spread over the year also.

6

WEBSITE DESIGN & CONTENT

6.1 INTRODUCTION

Having reviewed the various options for building the site itself, this chapter helps you to come up with good content for the website itself.

By far the most common use of a website for your business is to use it instead of, or alongside, a print brochure to tell potential customers all about your business. The site typically contains text and pictures giving information all about your business, and then has a 'Contact Us' page or form for customers to fill out to email or phone you for more information. The typical site may go so far as to allow customers to place a provisional booking on the site, but doesn't include a full shop or reservation system.

Requirements for an individual website are impossible to cover here, but below are some general rules to follow when creating your website specifications and design.

6.2 GENERAL RULES FOR WEBSITE DESIGN

The basic rules are:

- **Keep the site design simple and easy-to-navigate:** This is something that a good web developer will do anyway, but you should keep it in mind when choosing what navigation structure you will have on your site. You don't want visitors to have to click three times in order to find out what you do – that should be evident on the first page.

- **Don't overuse Flash:** Personally, I find sites using Flash that take ages to load (anything over 10 seconds) quite annoying and I will often leave the site in frustration. I know others feel the same. For a product such as photography or graphic design, Flash shows them off to great effect but, for most other sites, it's simply annoying. Use it in moderation for effect if you wish, but try not to get carried away.

- **Make sure the site is visually appealing, and easy on the eye:** I had a royal blue background with white writing on my first website – people found it hard to read! I changed it immediately.

- **Don't put music or sound files on your site:** They are not good if someone is visiting your site while at work, and can startle other visitors.

- **Don't put large, slow-loading graphics on your page:** I've lost count of the number of times I've left a site when it was saying 'Loading … 20%'. Reduce the size of your graphics easily using MS Paint! Open the picture using Paint, then go to Image > Resize / Skew, and reduce the size by percentage to the size you want.

- **Consider the sales process for your product:** How will customers purchase from your site? Will they buy samples first? Will they shop / search the site in a variety of ways? Accommodate as many alternatives as you reasonably can.

- **Make product descriptions clear, graphically detailed and, where suitable, personal** (whether you are selling tangible products, services, consultancy or anything else): Include a clear, well-taken photograph of each. When shopping, some people identify with words, others with pictures. It's a simple rule, but provide both.

- **Make contact information easy to find:** An easy-to-spot 'Contact Us' link available on every page of your site is vital. This is usually the next stage in the sales process for a visitor once they have viewed your site – and must be easy for them to do.

- **Consider having a phone number with a person at the end of it listed on your site:** How many hours have you spent on the other end of a voice-automated system, cursing it to high heaven? Unless you are an extremely large operation, if your market is focused on Ireland, and if it makes business sense to you, do consider having a human on the end of the phone if possible. For our sites, we field a lot of queries on the phone and, in many cases, we manage to secure business we would not otherwise get.

- **Provide returns / warranty information clearly:** This is required to get a merchant account anyway if you wish to be an online trader, but providing product information, shipping information (if relevant) and other site or store policies is simply good business practice.

6.3 CREATING SITE CONTENT

Planning your site content is the next phase of building a successful website. Discover the optimal niche for your website, find correct keywords and choose the most profitable website concept for you. Build your website structure so that it is optimal from the point of view of both human visitors and search engine spiders.

Before building your website, make sure you take some time to think through the kind of site you'd like, the content, the message you're sending and, if you have favourite sites already, the kind of look and feel you're after. The site may have a friendly, personable feel if the service or products you offer make people feel better, or you may want a businesslike, corporate look and feel to assure people of your professionalism.

The steps involved in planning your site content are:

- **Identify your market segment / niche:** Will your site be a shop, a portal or a brochure site? Identify your vertical market, too – are you in sports, manufacturing, professional services or entertainment? Spend some time researching websites in your area – whether they are Irish websites or further afield. Make a note of styles used, the ones you like and, if there's a site you particularly like, use it to inspire the design of your own.

- **Choose the keywords** that apply to your product and / or website. These are specific words or phrases used by customers to describe your product. There are several keyword tools out there, but none have a patch on Google's. It's worth signing up for an AdWords account just to use the keyword tool to choose keywords for the content of your site. See http://www.google.com/sktool/. You need to build all site content around the top five keywords you choose for your site to give you a better chance of being listed high up in search engine rankings for those keywords. If you have more than five keywords, analyse the ones that are most profitable for you and prioritise them. Later in the book, we'll look at using pay-per-click advertising instead in a situation like this.

- **Build the navigation of your site around these keywords:** If you sell five different products as your main business, these should each be on the left-hand menu, or on tabs across the top bar, to make them easy for customers to find.

- **Think about the style you'd like for your site:** Do you want to convey a corporate / business look, or something more personal? Do you want it to appear bright and fun, or muted and professional? Be aware that nearly all sites are built using a **template** for the look and feel, colour scheme and the navigation bars at the top, the left-hand and sometimes right-hand side of a site. Designing this template is often the lengthiest part of the website design process. Once in place, the rest of the site content can usually be added quite quickly.

If your website designer asks whether you want static or dynamic pages, the difference is that static pages are those on your site that are pre-compiled and don't change versus dynamic pages that are compiled on the fly.

Dynamic pages can customize the webpage to tailor it more closely to each user – for example, when someone viewing fashion items in a catalogue just wants to see those that are size 12, the page pulls up those items from the database and displays them on the page. Another example is when you visit Amazon and it says 'Welcome back, Aisling Mackey' – having picked up information stored in your browser's cookies and created the page on the fly. Dynamic pages provide great personalisation and also are the best solution for companies with large amounts of data (we have 3,000 products on our crafts site, for example – creating 3,000 different pages would take too long. Instead, a single template page is used and each time it creates the page on the fly, based on data it pulls up from the back end database.

While dynamic pages have some great features, at the present time search engines do not pick up on their content the way they do for static pages. This is being addressed, but it is a definite drawback of the technology.

7
MARKETING – ONLINE & OFFLINE

7.1 INTRODUCTION

Now that your website is built, the next step is getting the word out there so people know it exists. This chapter covers marketing your website through various different media. With my four sites, I think we've just about tried everything! The approximate breakdown of how we get our leads across our sites is shown below.

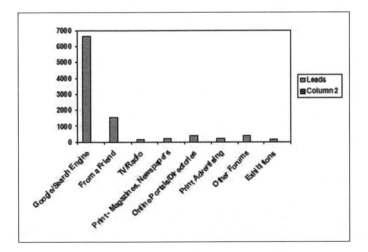

Figure 7.1: Breakdown of leads to our sites

For all my websites, our focus and spend is now on Internet marketing. Why? Because approximately **80%** of our leads come from Internet advertising (though this represents a smaller percentage of our annual spend – Google is excellent value for money).

Although we have been profiled and written up in every paper and magazine, and have been on several radio shows and TV, during the year that we had the most PR, we only got **6%** of our leads from it.

Our experience is that general PR is not as effective for niche markets and products, though it can work well for products with broader markets.

We no longer do any form of print advertising. The last year we did it – in relevant magazines and paper supplements – only **5%** of our leads came from it, although nearly 30% of our marketing budget that year was spent on it. For us – an online business in a niche area – it did not work well.

We get by far the greatest return on investment, as well as proportion of leads, from the Internet. It makes sense: we are an online company – and our customers are online, too!

7.2 SEARCH ENGINE OPTIMISATION

Search engine optimisation, or SEO, involves the use of various techniques to improve a website's ranking in search engine results and thus attract more visitors. In layman's terms, this means altering the content and other aspects of your website to raise your place in the rankings of Google and other search engines when people search for keywords relevant to your business.

How can I use SEO to improve the rankings of my website?
Getting your site listed in the top results in Google is often seen as the holy grail of Internet marketing success! SEO is the process of taking into account how search engines work, and what people search for when it comes to building content and other features of your website.

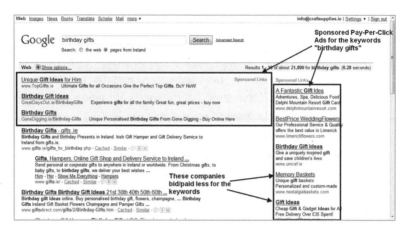

Figure 7.2: Winning the SEO war on Google search listings

None of the leading search engines – Google, Yahoo or Microsoft's Bing – reveal their ranking mechanisms, but the following steps have shown to be effective in practice:

- **Step 1:** Make sure the **metatags** on your site are filled out correctly. Metatags are in the code of your site and are used to provide a description to Google (or other search engines) of your site, and the keywords used to index it. If you go to the home page of your site and View > Source in your browser, you can see what the metatags for your site are.

Example: Amazon.co.uk's metatags:

<title>Amazon.co.uk: low prices in Electronics, Books, Music, DVDs & more</title>
<meta name="description" content="Low prices on digital cameras, MP3, LCD TVs, books, music, DVDs, video games, software, home & garden and much, much more. Free delivery on orders over £15." />
<meta name="keywords" content="digital camera, LCD TV, books, DVD, low prices, video games, pc games, software, electronics, home, garden, video, amazon" />

- **Step 2:** Be careful when choosing the **names of the pages** on your site. For example, a page named www.amazon.co.uk/toys/barbie.asp will be picked up as 'barbie' by search engine bots and served in the results for dolls and Australian picnics! Try to name your pages as accurately to their content as possible.

- **Step 3:** Choose the four or five **keywords** that define your business's products, services, USP. These are the words for which you wish to be listed in search engines results, so build the content on your website around these words. For Google to list your site as relevant for one of the words, the word needs to be listed approximately five times on one page – so, if you've chosen 'baby slings' as one of your keywords / phrases, you need to write the content of your home page to include that phrase at least five times if possible! Yes, this sounds hard to do – especially without making it too obvious – but that's what search engines rate on!

- **Step 4:** Ensure there are plenty of **links** to and from your site, since Google also places value on how 'connected' your site is. Register with free directories – this will increase the number of links to your site, and also you may show up quicker as part of these directories than you do without! And encourage partners to link to your site.

- **Step 5:** Add **multimedia content**. Search engines now rate sites with multimedia content such as videos, music or other interactive content over those without. Add a demo for your product (it doesn't have to be on the front page) or a podcast.

- **Step 6:** To register with Google, go to www.DMOZ.org, the open directory project used by Google for indexing the web. Be warned, it can take a long time to be added and, unless you have no links at all to your site, Google's bots should find you by then themselves. Note that Yahoo and AOL will charge you to register as a business with their search engine. Make sure to register with free web directories in your region / market area – for example, www.finditireland.com, www.browseireland.com, www.irish-guide.com – and any others you find.

And after all this, there still is no guarantee of top search engine rankings. The rankings the bots use to rate sites for relevance change all the time and your market and keywords may be extremely competitive. For these reasons, and the fact that we have many more than four or five keywords to be linked to, we use pay-per-click advertising primarily for my sites.

Note: If there is any content in your website that you do not wish to be used for search engine rankings, you can add instructions to the robots.txt file on your site regarding which areas in your website layout to avoid.

7.3 PAY-PER-CLICK ADVERTISING

Pay-per-click (PPC) advertising is adverts placed on search engine pages and content networks (sites such as blogs, portals and general web content) in which advertisers pay their host only when their ad is clicked. Search engine PPC is the most common, where advertisers typically bid on keyword phrases relevant to their target market.

The basic premises of pay-per-click are:

- **Only clicks on an advert are paid for**, not page impressions – so it doesn't matter how many times a person sees your ad, you only pay if and when they click on it.

- Advertisers choose **a set of words to bid on**.

- Advertisers set **daily budgets** for how much they're willing to spend on clicks in a day.

- Depending on what you and others are willing to pay for each click on a keyword, your listing will be slotted into the list of adverts in order – whoever is willing to pay the most to show up for the word 'Arsenal', for example, will be top of the list of ads.

To demonstrate how it works – below is a search for 'birthday gifts' on Google Ireland, on sites for Ireland.

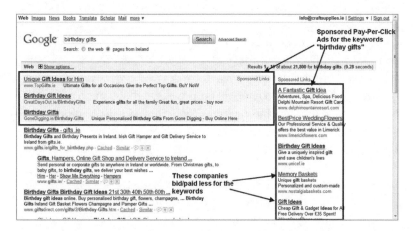

Figure 7.3: Search results for 'birthday gifts' on Google

Above are the results. The normal, non-advertised search results are in the section in the middle-left. The adverts are shown in the highlighted boxes. All of these adverts listings have set up Google AdWords pay-per-click accounts, and have bid on the words 'birthday gifts'. The listings at the top of the page were willing to pay the most to be there, and the amount each listing was willing to pay decreases as you go down the listings on the right-hand side.

How much you are willing to pay for a keyword someone has searched for determines your place in the listings for that word. Bear in mind, however, that you only pay that price if someone actually CLICKS on your ad – hence the term pay-per-click. You pay nothing to simply appear on the page, and will get many times more impressions on a page for a word than you will get clicks.

7.4 Setting Up a Pay-Per-Click Advertising Campaign

Start with the campaign settings on Google.

Select 'New Campaign' to start a new campaign. Then enter some basic information for the campaign settings:

- A **campaign name** – anything you like;

- The **geographical locations** you wish to target – here you can choose where your ad will be shown – for example, to browsers based in Ireland, the UK or both. Choose the location where your customers live – for most readers, this will be Ireland.

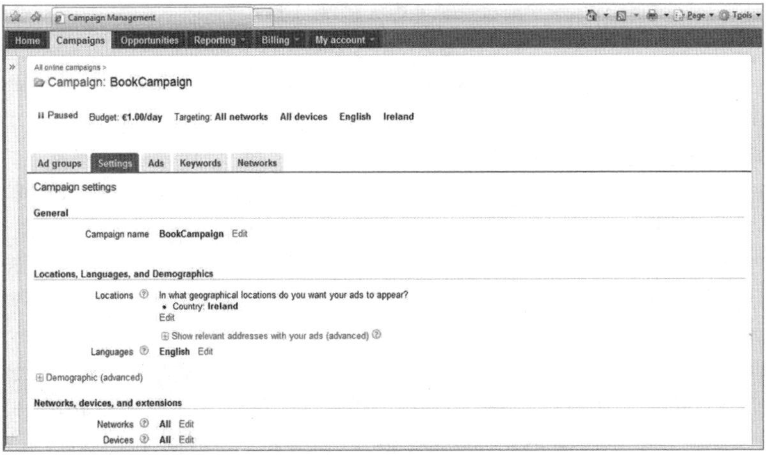

Figure 7.4: Setting up a Google AdWords campaign

Next choose the **language** your customers speak – the default is English. Then choose which kind of **devices and content** you want your ad to appear on:

- **Content:** You may have noticed that, often when reading a website, relevant ads will appear in the middle of the text of a web page, or on either side. By leaving this to the default, you allow your ad to appear on normal Google searches and also on its search partners as a sponsored ad at the top, left or right sides or within content. As an example, a lot of people might find my ad when they are reading a crafting blog that is displaying Google ads – because of the relevant content of the blog, Google displays my craft supplies shop ad as one of the targeted ads for that website.

- **Devices:** You also can allow ads to be shown on handheld devices, such as iPhones, as well as computers. If your site has a lot of multimedia or dynamic graphics content, you may want to exclude handheld devices if it won't display well, but otherwise it's fine to leave this set to the default.

I allow my ads to appear on all devices and content, and about one-third of my clicks are from ads that show up as syndicated content – in the middle of a relevant web page.

The next step is important – it's where you **set a daily budget for the maximum amount of money you want to spend on your Google AdWords campaign**. It's tempting to set this high so you don't miss any clicks, but you need to decide how much you are truly willing to pay each month, and divide and apply that on a per day budget. When enough clicks are clicked and your budget is reached, your site stops showing up on Google searches until the next day. I recommend starting low – for example, €1 per day. After a few days, you can check your clicks, see whether they are hitting your maximum limit each day, and up the limit if you can afford it. Google allows you to set particular days or time of day for your ads to show, to maximise impact – this is good if you find, or know, that your customers buy mostly at home at weekends (as is the case with my UK customers) or during the week (the norm with my Irish customers).

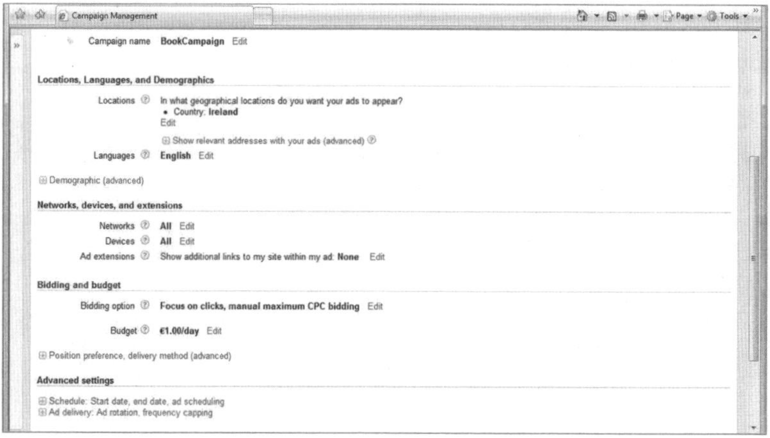

Figure 7.5: Setting a budget for your Google AdWords campaign

At this point there is **an option to set a default value for each word that you're willing to pay**. Google recommends leaving this until later and I second that – this is a more detailed process you should tackle on its own after you have the basic campaign set up.

OK, you now have a new campaign set up. This might be something like 'Christmas 2010', which will run for a few months, or it may be an ongoing campaign you use indefinitely to advertise your company and products.

Create your ad groups

Within a campaign, you can have several 'ad groups' running, to allow you to target different groups with different products and ads – for example, for a Christmas 2010 campaign for a book store, you may set up several ad campaigns – one for people searching for gifts for their mums, another for those looking to buy something for their spouse – and have different ads show up depending on whether they search for 'gift, mother' or 'gift, spouse' or something similar. Each of these can be a different ad group, showing different text in the ad itself, and also optionally having different landing pages for each ad group (the

different book store ads may bring you to different categories on their
site when you click on the ad).

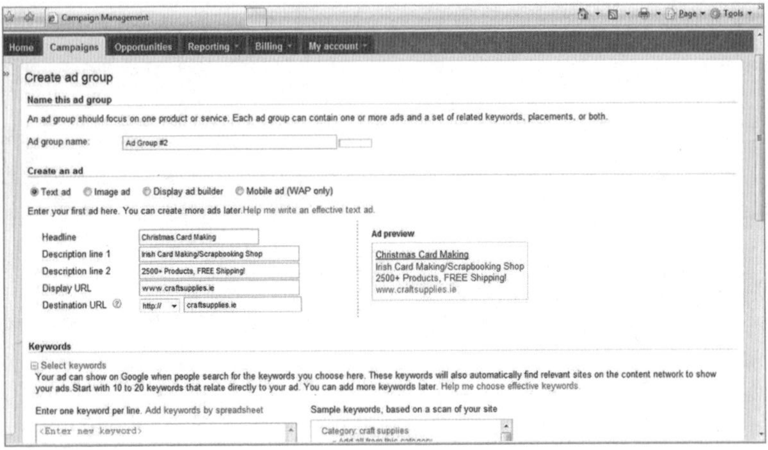

Figure 7.6: Creating an ad group for your Google AdWords campaign

The first thing to do is enter the actual text for your ad – as it will
appear to the customer on the screen. Google has rules and regulations
about how this text can be formatted: not too many exclamation marks
or symbols; pricing information recommended; also make sure to
include a strong 'call to action' in the text. All this helps to get the
customer to the next step, which is to click on your ad and visit your
site. An ad saying '10% off your first order!' is more likely to get a hit
than one with weak text and vague descriptions of products. Think
about what is unique to your business, and ensure that this is
communicated in the small amount of text available to you for your
Google ad. At the same time, don't try to cram too much – keep the
message simple.

Google Help provides excellent guidelines – and videos – to help
you craft this ad to provide the strongest punch.

Once you have created your ad, the next step is to **choose the keywords that you wish to bid on**. If someone searches for that keyword (for example, 'football') or a keyword phrase ('Irish football jersey'), your ad will show up as one of the ads listed on the page with the results from the search.

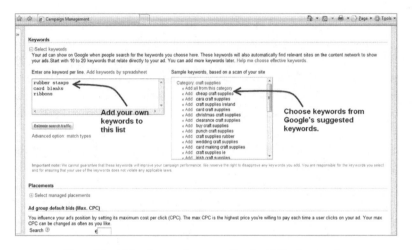

Figure 7.7: Adding keywords to your Google AdWords campaign

Google makes it very easy for you to select a large range of relevant keywords. I'll go into that in a moment but, before reviewing the suggested Google keywords, I recommend that you take a few minutes to jot down quickly a list of words you think your customers use to describe your products and / or business. While it is excellent at providing cross-referenced keywords, Google usually cannot pick up colloquialisms that may be unique to your country or even your own customer-base.

Placements

Below the keyword selection tools is a title, 'Placements'. In addition to showing up for general Google searches, many websites choose to host or contain Google ads within the content of their sites. This service is called Google AdSense. The sites hosting the ads earn a price-per-click for each click of an ad that occurs from their site. Mostly free or public sites – for example, message boards, club or group sites – use this to generate revenue. So, if you are on a message board chatting about sport, then the ads that will display on that site (usually at the top and bottom of the page) will be sport-related.

You can take advantage of this for your site by choosing specific websites (that use Google AdSense already to display ads) to target with your own Google ad. Do you know of any message boards, portals, or websites where the public congregate and have a community relevant to your business? Then add these sites to the Placements in Google.

The last part of the initial setup is setting your keyword maximum cost-per-click (Max CPC). In my experience of giving Internet business / marketing courses, this is the part of Google AdWords that most challenges new business owners. How can you be in the top two or three listings when people search, without going over budget? Remember our diagram (**Figure 7.3**) showing where businesses using Google AdWords / pay-per-click show up on Google searches:

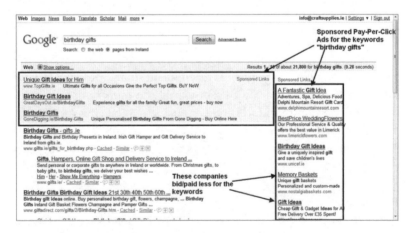

Figure 7.8: Search results for 'birthday gifts' on Google (Figure 7.4 repeated)

The more you bid for a keyword, the higher your listing will go. But I have found that being in the top three of the results for a specific keyword is often enough to generate a high rate of clicks through to my website. Many people make the mistake of continuing to raise the amount they are willing to pay-per-click on each keyword until they get to the #1 position on the listings – on every listing, on every keyword. This often costs a lot more than being listed second or third. I don't know about you, but when I'm searching for something on the Internet, it's rare to find it with the first click, and if I do, I usually check out a couple more relevant websites to make sure I'm getting value for money, the best rate of shipping, etc. So I click, not only on the first listed ad but also on the second, third and so on – so do most other people.

My recommendations for choosing the best bidding level for each of your keywords are:

- **Work out your budget:** How much can you afford to spend per month, per week and per day. Set up that amount in Google. Once you hit this spend each day, your ads will cease to appear and your budget will not be exceeded.

- **Start all your keywords at a low base rate:** For example, 5c per click. A few minutes later, check the keywords in your account to see whether any of them are showing up as 'Below first page bid'. If they have, this means that your bid is too low for them to be in the top 10 of businesses bidding on that keyword. If the keyword is one of your core words to describe your business, increase it by 5c or 10c and review it again a few minutes later.

- **Check your ad placements manually:** Continue until you are happy with the position of your ads, but remember, the more you pay per click, the fewer clicks you will receive for your budget. As you increase your CPCs, check who you're up against and how their ads look by going to www.google.ie (if you are advertising in Ireland) and doing a search for your own keywords. Mark down where your ad appears for each of your words – and which you are happy with, which not. Keep checking as you increase your CPCs. Make sure that you use your money wisely, and that you spend the most money on the keywords that most closely describe your business and products to maximise the clickthroughs and resulting sales.

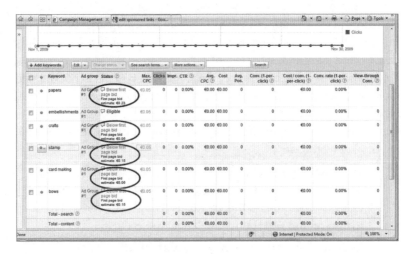

Figure 7.9: Checking your ad placements

I checked the campaign above just five minutes after I had submitted the keywords with initial Max CPCs of just 5c. The ones in bold were showing up on page 2 or 3 of the results; the others were showing up on the first page. My ads were not at the top of the list on the first page yet, but a few iterations of increasing the CPCs a few cents at a time, and they were.

Sometimes on Google AdWords two businesses bid on the same keyword, both with a high CPC – for example, one at €2 per keyword, the other at €2.10. This means both are willing to pay up to €2 (or €2.10) in order to appear in the top listings of search results for a particular search keyword. What can happen here is that the businesses get into a bidding war which inflates how much is paid in order to come at the top of the ad listings. Both businesses bid against each other, going all the way up to €2.10, when finally one of the businesses loses and takes second place. Assume that the next highest bidder has set 50c as their highest CPC. In this scenario, they will pay just 50c to appear in position #3, while the others pay four times that amount. If either of the high bidders were to drop their bid down to 60c, they could get into position #2 for a fraction of the cost.

Google's recommended max CPC tends to be based on the existing highest bidder's max CPC. If, instead of using Google's suggested amount, you increase your lowest CPC gradually until you are high in the listings, you can avoid paying an artificially inflated price.

How much can you expect to pay per keyword? The answer to this depends on the competitiveness of your market sector – for example:

- **Low level of competition:** As a craft supplies shop advertising on Google Ireland, there is not much competition to bid against – just a handful of competitors – so the cost of showing up in the top three results for craft-related words is quite low – usually less than 30c.

- **High level of competition:** If you check out the wedding stationery market in the UK, and search for 'wedding stationery' in the UK, more than 10 pages of advertisers show up. Over 100 advertisers, all bidding on the keyword 'wedding stationery'! So, to make an impression in the UK would mean paying at least €1.00 per click, in order to appear on the first page.

When I researched a UK AdWords campaign, the price for showing up on the front page of keywords such as wedding, stationery, invitations, etc. was just too high. Also, my site specialises in DIY wedding stationery, where couples print and assemble their own stationery and save lots of money in the process. I decided to set up phrases in Google as my keywords, rather than just individual words, to target my customers more closely and get better value for money on my clicks. It meant narrowing the search beyond just 'wedding stationery' to what we specialise in – DIYing your invitations – but it also meant a more closely targeted customer, more likely to buy from my site.

If I set up a phrase in AdWords as '"DIY wedding stationery" (with the double quotes), Google will only show my ad if ALL the words are Googled together and in the order I have given; without the double quotes, Google will show my ad if ANY of the words 'DIY', 'wedding' or 'stationery' are used in any order, and not always together. In this way, I was able to narrow down my target audience by using more specific phrases as keywords instead of simple individual words. I got more clicks from better prospects / customers on the web. My sales increased, and my AdWords budget decreased.

Measuring campaign effectiveness

Next, there are several ways to measure the effectiveness of Google campaigns:

- **Google Analytics:** Google offers basic information on your AdWords campaign after a short time lag, and this information shows you how many times your ad has been displayed, how many clicks you received, for which words, the average amount spent per click and lots of other information as well. If you go a little further and embed some Google Analytics code in your site, Google then can provide you with further detail on how many completed transactions originated from Google, demographical information on visitors to your site, and much more.

- **Other analytics packages:** StatCounter.com is a free analytics package used by over two million users. It was created by an Irishman and is still based here, and in some cases provides you with more detail than Google, with the benefit of proper support (Google provides only FAQs).

- **Measure during account sign-up on your own website:** When people sign up to our websites, they have to choose from a dropdown menu to tell us how they found us. We have some basic statistics to go with the package, but this feature allows us to add new lead generating activities and then measure easily (although approximately) which are performing the best.

The analytics available to you to measure your marketing campaigns are one of the fantastic things about Internet business and marketing – it is extremely measurable – you can see exactly how you're spending your money, what's working, and what's not.

7.5 OTHER ONLINE ADVERTISING & MARKETING

Web portals and directories

Another good source for marketing and advertising are **web portals and online directories**. I mentioned these at the beginning of the book – they are websites that provide lots of information from different sources in a single website. Apart from the standard search engine features, web portals offer other content-related services such as forums, articles, news and other information. IGoogle, MyYahoo!, MSN are all examples of portals used by the public every day. For my markets, the WeddingsOnline site in Ireland is the main wedding portal – offering a supplier directory, shop, forums, articles and other information all about planning a wedding. Because it provides so much information to help brides and grooms, www.weddingsonline.ie receives nearly 150,000 visits per month. These people are my desired target audience, and it's a good place for me to advertise to them. When choosing a web portal on which to advertise your site, make sure to always check the number of visits the site gets per month and, if it's possible to find out, how many of these are in your customer category.

TIP: A €50 subscription for a year's entry on web directory sounds more tempting than one for €200, but you may get only five leads from the first and 500 from the latter. Check out their relevant traffic.

Online message boards / forums

More common than portals but with less content are the plethora of online message boards or chat forums on the Internet. These cover a wide range of topics – we have a busy one ourselves on our crafts site. **Boards.ie** and **Askaboutmoney.ie** are two very well-known Irish message boards.

Many people visit their favourite message boards on a daily basis, and most message boards pay for their hosting costs using Google AdSense ads on their site. Some even have their own advertising options set up – sites such as **magicmum.com**, which has a 'GoShopping' page with Irish web shops on it, all paying to advertise.

Figure 7.10: The "Go Shopping" page on the **MagicMum.com** *message board. This message board is run as a non-profit, but some time back, the owner was struggling to cover hosting costs with AdSense profits. I suggested a page with Irish web shops that would appeal to Irish mums. She liked it, launched it, and it worked very well indeed.*

If there's a message board in your niche market, these are usually worth advertising with, as long as the package they offer is reasonable relative to how many visits they get per day, week and month (compare against clicks from Google or readership of magazines).

TIP: Some forums and portals will allow you to post in either all or a specific section of their message board, once you take out an advertisement with the site. This can be invaluable – if you can post up and get board members talking about you, the viral / word-of-mouth marketing is worth a hundred ads. Always ask if this comes with the package when buying an ad with one of these websites.

When starting out with no budget for marketing at all, join message boards in your own product area of expertise. While you are not allowed to advertise directly, some forums will allow you to post / reply helpfully to questions asked, while having your website link in your signature or by using a distinctive name. In the early days, you can start a trickle of clicks to your website as you post helpful information up on the message board – hopefully for people who need it and will notice it.

Blogs
Blogs have been a buzzword for the last number of years. Short for 'weblog', a blog is essentially an online diary where authors write publicly about their lives, opinions, beliefs and thoughts, and, in the case of a business blog, about their business, products and services and the market they are in at large. In 2008, there were 200 million+ blogs in the world, and that number is expected to hit 1 billion in 2010. While the hype has been big, from a business perspective only a handful have worldwide recognition and are making a full time living through advertising on their blog or other revenue streams. Blogs like the Huffington Post (www.huffingtonpost.com), boingboing.com or techcrunch.com are rare examples of hugely successful blogs. Many of

the top blogs are of a technical slant and, although so many abound, there is still a sense that the whole 'blog' concept hasn't hit the world at large properly just yet.

I must admit that I feel that the world is made up of people who were born to blog, and those who will always feel a little uncomfortable with the idea in general. Perhaps it is the introvert / extrovert divide! I set up a blog that did very well in its first year, but it turned out, and I wasn't too surprised, that I am not one of the group born to blog. I feel vaguely embarrassed at the idea of putting my personal ideas out there on a daily basis, and didn't enjoy creating and posting up articles – it felt like more work to me. The majority of blogs die a quiet death after three months or so, but for those that don't, it's often a fantastic platform to publicise your business and ideas, craft yourself a following, and gain publicity through it all.

However, the reality is that, for most people, making a full living from a blog is about as likely as becoming a supermodel. What blogs can do is to enhance your position in search listings, and to help you to draw an audience you may not otherwise attract.

A friend of mine writes about technology and gadgets for one of the national broadsheets, and has a blog on which he occasionally reviews various electronics and gadgets. One week, he reviewed a particular camera – we'll call it the 'Canon ABC'. He added the review to his blog. A week later, he was submitting a piece on the camera to the paper, and wanted to check some technical details on the camera, and so he Googled the camera name. The first site that came up in the search results? His own blog. In this way, a blog provides a medium that is extremely easy to add content to without the hassle of updating your website, and enables you to show up in more search results than you would otherwise.

If you want to start a business blog, it's a good idea to embed the blog in your own business website, so any clicks it picks up on search engines will be directed to your main site. All the major blogging tools – www.wordpress.com, www.blogger.com, and www.typepad.com – provide the option to host on their site or your own.

On many blogging tools, setting up the blog is free. Sometimes, there are additional charges – for example, to use better-looking templates for your site or other features – but, overall, a blog costs little to set up other than your time.

Figure 7.11: My blog! http://chewingpaper.typepad.com

Do think about whether you have enough content and interest in writing a blog to make it sustainable over time. Also, does the idea of blogging actually appeal to you? Nearly all the crafters on my forums have blogs now. I was one of the last ones to add a blog, and I set up a business blog, not a personal one. My blog can be seen at http://chewingpaper.typepad.com. If you happen to visit, you may notice it has not been updated since 2008. At the end of the day, I'm not a blogger, nor do I have much free time to add new posts. However, I have got more than a handful of new customers via my blog and, had I kept updating it, I'm confident I would have received more.

Blogs are very much on the increase in Ireland, and the annual Irish Blog Awards is a fun night. Sites such as **www.beaut.ie** or **20major.net** are doing well. **IceCreamIreland.com**, on which there is a case study in **Chapter 8** in this book, do consistently well at the Irish Blog Awards. I first heard of them while attending the show. The company has attracted a whole new following through the IceCreamIreland blog, which enabled Kieran Murphy to launch a book off the back of it.

Facebook

Using viral marketing in Facebook has worked really well for us. Our export market is 10% and growing – mainly because of our Facebook page and following. We've had huge impact from that.
Daragh Murphy, CEO, HairyBaby.com

Facebook allows businesses to create a free Facebook page within their site. Other Facebook users can choose to be become a fan of the page, and to receive any updates the business posts up as part of its status updates. This works best for businesses that have products with a cult following or a product on which they can easily provide updates and information to fans. Like message boards, many of these pages fall flat on their face when they fail to garner a decent enough following, or, like a blog, the owners fail to update them regularly enough.

Whatever the downsides, these pages are free, reason enough to try it out anyway. We will be launching a Facebook page for our crafts site soon – we have many avid crafters who love to receive any titbits on new products, techniques or information. To try and make sure it stays active, I've drafted in some volunteers from my crafting message board to post up titbits of information each week, or pictures of creations they've made with our products. By spreading the workload, I'm hoping we can keep the page going longer and also attract more fans!

Twitter

So many ways of getting the message out, so little time. Twitter is the latest of the platforms hyped up for enabling communication in real-time between people. Although Twitter was originally intended for communication among individuals, a number of organisations have begun to actively participate on the platform. In some ways, Twitter is like real-time micro-blogging. Instead of lengthy posts, the person twittering posts a quick update, comment or status – usually just a line or two long – you have a maximum of 140 characters for your 'tweet'. Listeners can subscribe to different feeds that they are interested in, and then receive the tweets from those feeds on their phone or computer. Twitter is exciting and gives the world a real-time voice, but it can be tricky filtering out the quality content from the bad.

Businesses use Twitter in different ways. Some tweet directly themselves, using the channel as a direct marketing tool; some have their employees tweet with their corporate hat on; other businesses use Twitter to find out what people think of **them**, too. New applications are coming onto the market to enable businesses to listen out for their name and what's being said about them. Big Brother is listening but, if your competitors are listening, then you probably want to, too.

7.6 THE ONE-OFF SALES MODEL

In the next section, we'll look at viral marketing, referrals and repeat business, which is what most online businesses are seeking to achieve. The one-off sales model is much rarer, but comes into play on our DIYWedding site. To date, we've not seen much repeat business when it comes to weddings. Each bride / groom usually will purchase from us a handful of times in the lead-up to their wedding – so, in that sense, we see repetition but, after that, the customer is gone for the foreseeable future. How can we maximise the window of opportunity during that time to encourage referrals?

The main focus we used on our wedding site was to take a lot of the domain knowledge we had on creating wedding stationery and put it to good use by providing free templates, suggested wordings, lists of fonts, FAQs, information resources, links to useful articles, etc. All of this increases our rankings in Google and also increases traffic through search engines to the site for brides looking for invitation templates, etc. Traffic leads to sales, and sales leads to happy owners. It's worked for us and we get tons of mentions on the wedding forums for our free resources, too.

7.7 VIRAL MARKETING

On our websites, the next biggest lead generator after Google is 'Referred by a friend' – at nearly 25%. Referrals only ever come from a happy customer, as does repeat business, both of which you need in order to persist and be successful on the Internet.

A happy customer, in my experience, usually comes down to good customer service, a feeling of value for money, happiness with the product and on the Internet – good customer management. By that, I mean providing additional features on your site that go a little above and beyond the usual for a business of your kind. Why do you need to do that? It goes back to the highly competitive and increasingly-fickle nature of online shopping. Another shop is just a click away – how do you encourage referrals and repeat business to YOUR website?

For my websites, referrals are important on both my retail sites – but, for my wedding site, we don't get much repeat business. However, we do get a lot of referrals from happy customers which, according to them, comes from quick service and turnout times, great value for money and a unique product in our DIY stationery kits, which help them save money. Although we can't get repeat business, we do offer lots of freebies on the site – free MS Word templates for a huge range of designs, guidelines for printing on different cards and papers, suggestions for wordings for their invites. Our goal is to make customers feel looked after and it works.

For our crafts site, we do a lot of work to maintain our customer-base and encourage them to shop with us on a regular basis. We compete with approximately five other sites in Ireland, and carving out a USP on the web in a market like this is difficult. We offer a unique set of products, as we have a unique set of suppliers that it has taken me many, many hours and days to find. We offer a fast, reliable service. On top of that, we currently offer our customers:

- **A free message board** to chat to other crafters – approximately 250,000 messages posted so far. I also use this message board to poll the 1,000 or so members on new product lines I'm considering, to ask their opinion on almost anything and, of course, to advertise any new products we've introduced. The forum runs on free software, and is cheap to host.

Figure 7.12: An online class on our craftsupplies.ie message board.

- **Free online classes** in crafts provided through the chat forum.
- **Free shipping** over a certain amount purchased on the site;
- In the past, we also had a **project team** who made cards / scrapbook pages using our products each month but, for us,

the return on investment couldn't justify it continuing – we simply weren't getting the sales on the products being used, but this idea does work well for many other crafts businesses;

- We also provide listings for **crafts classes** around the country and a customer gallery;

- We introduce new products every week, to keep things fresh!

7.8 NEWSLETTERS

As an online business, **email newsletters** are one of the most powerful marketing tools available to you. They're cheap, easy-to-send, and have direct impact on sales

For sites seeking repeat business, I would recommend sending a **newsy monthly newsletter** with as much rich content as possible. If you provide baby products, perhaps mention recent interesting research into babies! If you provide music products, mention concerts coming up. In all cases, provide indirect information that is relevant to the customer to create a positive brand image of your company as the expert in its domain, especially useful information to customers that isn't necessarily about sales.

Here are some guidelines for sending email newsletters:

- Make sure your customers have '**opted in**' to receive communication from you – if you use a rented / purchased list, make sure that the list-members have chosen to receive communication.

- Have a 'Subscribe to our newsletter' link on the front page of your site to catch any leads.

- Personalise the newsletter, if you can.

When you first send to a newsletter customer list, expect reasonably high **bounce-back** rates – perhaps 20% to 30% for first-time mailshots.

This will fall to 2% to 5% from a list regularly emailed and 5% to 15% for a list mailed less than monthly.

Unsubscribe rates are similar: 1% to 2% for frequently emailed lists; 2% to 5% for less than once a month contact. The more you send newsletters, the more you hone your list to people who genuinely wish to receive them.

There are two main methods for sending out an email – send it yourself using an email client, or send it using one of several online email marketing tools.

The advantages of using an online email marketing tool (for example, **www.verticalresponse.com**) are that they:

- Provide open / read / click-through statistics to enable you measure exact response.
- Are easy-to-use and set-up.

However, the disadvantages are that they charge a small fee per email to send the newsletter out.

The advantages of using your own email editor are that it's free and quick to use, with no new system to be learnt. However, the downsides are that:

- It doesn't provide open / read / click-through information.
- Your ISP may impose restrictions on when bulk emails can be sent out.

A general rule of thumb on the best time to send out a newsletter is:

- If your newsletter is read at work, send it on Wednesday or Thursday between 11am and 4pm;
- If your newsletter is primarily read at home and focuses on spare-time activities, send it on Sunday;
- Most people agree it's a good idea to send the newsletter out on the same day / time each month.

We send all our newsletters between Tuesday and Thursday, 11am to 4pm. We've found that's what works best for us

Now the hard question – what do I put in the newsletter? As with any marketing proposal, for a customer to take notice, the vendor must be able to offer **good value**, **uniqueness of product**, or **fill a customer need**. The recipients of your email are busy and you have approximately three to five seconds of their time as they glance at your email to capture their attention. Customers will glance at the first items in your newsletter and decide whether they wish to read on. You need to capture their attention immediately.

To capture their attention:

- **Always include a clearly-positioned and well-displayed special offer of some kind:** This may be a special product promotion, special offer, discount or enticing competition, as long as it is something of special **value** to the customer. This makes the email 'sticky' and greatly increases the chances of the reader clicking through to your website.

- **Keep headlines clear:** They should 'jump off' the page;

- **Include a summary at the top of the newsletter:** Use links to the various sections below.

- **Include rich content in your newsletter:** Add useful information, as well as marketing material, so the customer feels it is a genuine newsletter and does not discard it without viewing. What is 'rich content' depends on your customer-base and product-type but, for example, we include free projects in each newsletter, special offers, and useful information like last posting dates for Christmas or upcoming card holidays!

- **Include information about new products or blog additions:** Anything to show your site is lively, constantly updated, interesting and worth visiting.

7.9 PR & Press Releases

The effectiveness of a press release in publicising your company very much depends on the market that you are in. For my businesses, we are in several distinct niche markets – with crafters being one audience, brides and grooms another. Because of this, I have found PR to be effective primarily when closely targeted to a specific market. When we launched DIYWedding and were featured in every newspaper, magazine and radio station we could think of, and were on TV twice, only 6% of the customers we earned that year came from PR. (I think the real number may be higher though, as many people who said they heard about the site "From a friend" may have seen us on television.)

For products that apply to all walks of life – for example, music, sport, etc – the benefit from PR has the potential to be much greater. Either way, sending out a press release is free publicity that can be done using only the cost of time and no money, and is worth trying at least once for everyone.

If there is one point I'd like to make when it comes to writing press releases, it's to provide the journalist with an easy hook for writing a story. That means instead of sending out a press release announcing the launch of your website / business, you provide an angle about it that makes an easy story. Here are some tips for writing an effective press release:

- **Put a time / date stamp on the left hand side and the words 'For Immediate Release' at the top of the page** if the piece may be used immediately by journalists. If you want the journalist not to use the content until a specific date, such as your company launch or a public holiday, the release should say 'For Release 13 June' or similar.

- **A title:** This is vitally important in catching the attention of the journalist reading it. Make the title as catchy as possible – for our DIYWedding release, which was announced shortly after a wedding survey showing couples were spending more money than ever, we used: 'DIYWedding: New Irish Online Wedding

Company Saving Couples Thousands'. Perhaps a little cheesy, very direct, but it worked.

- Journalists don't want to hear that your company has launched – they want to hear **why what you're telling them is relevant to their readers**:
  - ○ **The first 'announcement' paragraph** summarises your story in three or four sentences – this enables the journalist to read the first paragraph and, from it, glean a good understanding of what the release is about. Make sure to include clearly what is unique about your product or service offering – are you the first of your kind, the best, or the only one out there?
  - ○ **The body of the press release** adds several short paragraphs, giving more detail on the first paragraph. Adding a quote is a good idea – for example, "Couples are getting into debt of over €10,000 to fund their weddings. At DIYWedding, we try to save them as much money as we can – by enabling them to make their own wedding stationery and other accessories with ease", said Aisling Mackey, owner of DIYWedding;
  - ○ **The closing paragraph** gives general background on the company and contact details for journalists to follow-up.
- **Provide a 'hook' to make it easy for journalists to write a story.** Give the journalist some context for your announcement – any recent news topics, a relevant survey perhaps. Why would people want to hear about your product? When launching our DIYWedding site, we sent out a press release including a recent study showing Irish couples were getting into debt up to €10,000. We then broadcast how we could save couples between €500 and €3,000. The result? Copy in the *Irish Times Magazine, Irish Independent, Daily Mail, Image, Irish Star*, a piece on Pat Kenny's radio show, Newstalk, RTÉ and TV3.

One of the first press releases I sent out was for my Cara Craft Supplies site. I sent out a pack to journalists with a simple, stylish, handmade card and materials inside to make a replica. The headline for the release was 'Make this card in less than one minute for 50c'. We received our first media mention from this release and made it into two magazines – the day I got that first call from a journalist was a great day and definitely a milestone for my business.

Various lists of contacts for distributing press releases can be found on the web such as www.przone.ie – a distribution site for press releases that charges approximately €85 to send your first press release with them. Another site, www.get2press.ie, charges just €40 (exc. VAT) to send your first press release with them but, in both cases, what matters is the quality and quantity of press contacts the company has in your area. Contact them before registering, to find out how many contacts they have in your particular niche. There are many .coms that provide a press release service but, unless they're based in Ireland, they're unlikely to have relevant contacts in the Irish press.

For my sites, I took a more home-grown and simple approach that took about a day of my time:

- Buy copies of all the newspapers (local and national) and magazines that you'd like to be featured in. There may be more than one type – when publicising www.budgetwedding.ie, we bought copies of newspapers and magazines relevant to both the wedding market and to finance and budgeting.

- Read through the papers and find the names of journalists writing on your subject.

- Work out their email addresses based on the syntax used by the publication – for example, firstname.lastname@newspaper.ie.

- Where you cannot work out email addresses for particular journalists, telephone the main phone number for each publication and ask the receptionist /switchboard or contact in the newsroom for the email addresses of the journalist – these are usually freely given out, as the journalists are trading in news and want to receive any relevant emails.

- Next, search online for TV stations, radio stations, any forums, portals or other online media and find email addresses in the same way as before, and add them to your list.

There is no hard and fast answer to when is the best time to send a press release. Generally speaking, sending a press release early in the week, and in the morning, is considered to be the best time, particularly for daily publications. For weekly publications, sending on a Friday can work well, as deadlines tend to run Sunday to Thursday. Don't send press releases over Christmas or other holidays, and avoid sending them if there is a major news item currently absorbing the nation or world (for example, Princess Diana's death, Barack Obama winning the US election).

The majority of journalists prefer to receive press releases by email – it's the easiest and quickest way for them to be read and sorted. Attachments are not preferred – include all content in the email message itself. HTML messages are OK, but plain text is preferred. This makes it easiest for the journalists to cut and paste for any pieces they may write.

7.10 OFFLINE MARKETING

I purposefully haven't mentioned much about offline marketing in this book for two reasons – it's well covered in non-Internet business books and, in my experience, it doesn't work well for most online businesses. Specifically:

- **Print advertisements:** Magazines, newspapers and supplements, local and national – while they attract some interest, the cost per lead relative to using Google instead doesn't even compare. If you do advertise, make sure that the publication goes out to your niche market. Otherwise, Google every time.

- **Trade shows and exhibitions:** We have done lots of these: general ones, niche ones, Irish ones, UK ones. Packing up the stock, handing out the flyers, standing up for hours on end. Without exception, they are expensive and exhausting. And, without exception, they don't give anywhere close to the value for money that online marketing does. We no longer do these shows, except in one case – if we are launching a new website or initiative, and we want to make a stir about it. Then, they can be useful to generate an initial buzz and help to brand the new website publicly – they are good for initial branding / word-of-mouth.

8

SUCCESSFUL IRISH INTERNET BUSINESSES

In this chapter are the results of six interviews I carried out with successful Irish Internet entrepreneurs. I have tried to cover as many business models as possible, so we have:

- A **manufacturer** who manufactures in Ireland, sells online and refuses to sell into shops (Daragh Murphy, HairyBaby.com).

- A **serial online entrepreneur** with a service website and a subscription one and others in the making (Derek Quinn, MovieExtras.ie and MyAddress.ie).

- The owner of **one of Ireland's best-known websites** and successful property portals in property (Eamonn Fallon, Daft.ie).

- A former accountant who balances home and work life and not one, but three arms of her businesses – **retail, trade and now manufacturing** (Maebh Collins, TheNaturalBabyResource.com).

- A **blogger**, who has managed to launch another product as a result of his blog following (Kieran Murphy, IceCreamIreland.com).

- An entrepreneur who started his business at the age of 16 and now has two million users for his **downloadable product** (Aodhán Cullen, StatCounter.com).

Each of these entrepreneurs tell us how they started, what steps they took, what they've learned. I have tried to keep the cases studies as 'real' as possible – no theories, just practice. This chapter is my favourite part of the book!

8.1 DARAGH MURPHY, CEO, HAIRYBABY.COM

Figure 8.1: HairyBaby.com

Online business type:
T-shirt manufacturer and online shop.

Website description:
Manufacturer and online retailer of funny Irish t-shirts and hoodies for men, ladies, kids and babies.

Were you always an entrepreneurial spirit?
No! I was a sound engineer by trade, and was in that market for seven or eight years. I was working as an audio-visual technician and DJ in Dublin for quite a while. But I always had a fascination with t-shirts. I would buy a new one each week before DJing. I always noticed what

others wore, too. As time went on, it was harder and harder to buy t-shirts. I found that the content on t-shirts that were available around Dublin was getting very lewd and crude! The Porn* brand was very popular – but they are gone now – they saturated the market and now no one wants to wear them anymore. I started to find it impossible to buy a new shirt every week. And I kept thinking: wouldn't it be great to get a cool Irish t-shirt? I kept waiting for one to arrive, but no one did it. And I had loads of cool ideas in my head.

What made you take the leap to set up yourself?

A few things happened that pushed me towards setting up myself. My wife got a transfer to Cork. I decided to stop my 9 to 5 work week, together with four nights DJing, and try Cork instead. I was poached and offered a job there, but it didn't work out and, after a month, I quit and decided to try my t-shirt idea.

How did you go about starting up?

I had no experience in the rag trade. While I was researching, I started DJing a few nights a week as well. I did a whole year's research on how to make t-shirts – web research, printing and packaging tradeshows, learning all about materials, methods. I bought 60+ shirts from around the world to see what packaging they came in, how quickly they delivered, the quality of the t-shirts, the branding they used. During this time, I did a business plan but was refused funding by the banks. I did a second one and was refused again. I was also turned down by the Enterprise Boards. No one seemed to 'get' our model – making and selling t-shirts online. It was too alien to them.

Did you ask family or friends to help with funding?

No. They had done enough to help already and I didn't want to put my family in that position.

What did you do next?
With no funding behind me, I had to start small. I started with six t-shirt designs. I bought in some stock blank t-shirts from UK. I found a screen-printer in Cork to print up my designs, and I sold to some shops in Cork. One shop had a delivery in the morning and called me in the afternoon as they'd sold six already and needed more stock. I grew the business organically. The initial sales to shops were great market validation. I wasn't making much money at this point, but I was generating cashflow to grow the company. I continued to work at night. At the end of year one (December 2004), we launched the website and I purchased our own printing machinery.

What option did you choose for getting your site built? An Irish web house, foreign developers, independent developer or build yourself?
My brother is a graphic designer. He and his company did the front end graphic design as well as the back end shop and, because he was my brother, they gave me a great deal. The first site cost €8,000.

How does your current site compare?
Our current site cost €45,000! We have a fantastic back end and the online shop has a lot of dynamic features. You can click on a t-shirt and then view it in other colours with mouse pass-overs. There's lots of dynamic HTML and server-side programming there to make it what it is today.

What shopping cart software do you use? Which payment gateway?
We use Custom Cart software. We used to use WorldPay for payments, but now use Realex. WorldPay delay payment to your account for weeks, which became impossible to support; Realex offer an expensive, but excellent, service.

How many people do you currently employ?
We currently employ six people.

What was your first premises? And where do you work from now?
When we started out in Cork, we were in a shed in my parents' house. We moved to a small office of about 700 sq ft after about a year. We then took a 1600 sq ft premises, and are now in 5,000 sq ft.

What shipping method do you use?
We use An Post, normal and courier post.

Is much of your business export? Are many of your orders overseas?
Yes – 10% and growing. Export is growing a lot – mainly because of our Facebook page and following. We've had huge impact from that.

Have you started any other entrepreneurial ventures since beginning HairyBaby.com?
Yes. We've started our second venture – HairyBabyAtWork. We specialise in providing organic t-shirts with logos for corporations. We're also looking at a carbon neutral t-shirt. These t-shirts are still high quality, but cheaper to buy.

What marketing methods do you use for your websites? PR? Newsletters? Pay-per-click? Print ads? Web portals? Tradeshows?
Newsletters work quite well. We have sent out press releases. We used MediaLive to send the press releases out. We've sent PR people out a pack with a shirt inside it. We've done, and continue to do, key tradeshows. The Ploughing Championships work well for us – we take a big stall. We are pulling out of web portals and corporate portals with discount schemes. We don't do print advertising; it doesn't work. We don't use Google AdWords, but we do use Facebook ads.

Other than Facebook, have you done any other work on building a community around your customers – for example, a blog, message board, newsletters, etc.?
Using viral marketing in Facebook has worked really well for us. One of our staff is responsible for monitoring our page and updating it

several times a day. We have fantastic fans and great support. We don't have a blog. I don't know much about it! No message board / chat forum either. Word-of-mouth is the best form of advertising, and has been put to good use in Facebook.

What has helped to set you apart from other, similar businesses (where applicable)? What is your Unique Selling Point?
We offer fundamentally modern IRISH humour, but nostalgia as well. Our products are a welcome alternative to the Blarney Stone for Irish buyers. The shops are polluted with cheap 'Oirish' products. We offer an alternative to that.

What do you imagine, or know, to be the biggest hurdle customers have to make to make a purchase on your site – for example, paying for shipping, not seeing the product in person first, struggling with using an online shopping cart?
A lot of it is about education. People don't trust the Internet with their credit card. After the first purchase, it is easier.

Have you considered opening a bricks-and-mortar shop as well? If not, why not?
I don't know. It's in the back of my mind to open one in Cork. We will road-test in our new premises, with a shop at the front. I like to do everything in baby steps. I have never gone the route of selling my t-shirts through a shop, although I am constantly approached. There are a few reasons why I never have:

- I feel that collecting money from shops is too hard. Shops take minimum of 90 days to pay – it is a total nightmare. Cashflow is king.

- I put a lot of research into what HairyBaby is before starting. I have seen distributors destroy a clothing label. I saw one who took a label and distributed to 300 shops all over Ireland. The market was flooded and soon demand for those t-shirts dried up and the manufacturer disappeared. I am protecting my brand. I want to avoid saturating the market as was done by this clothing label. I want to protect my staff. People jump in out of excitement and greed.

What are the advantages of working for yourself against working for someone else?
I love it. I love the fact that I can be outside of my building for an hour on the phone and no one can say anything to me. I can work when I want, though I'm first in, last out, but that will change! It does bring about an enormous amount of stress – especially when you have employees with mortgages. I have grown up a lot in the last five years!

Have you any words of advice for people considering setting up their own business?
Do it. BUT don't start your own business unless you have researched your business first. Research your market and that will tell you whether to start your own business or not.

8.2 DEREK QUINN, CEO, MOVIEEXTRAS.IE & MYADDRESS.IE

Online business type:
Online subscription model for MovieExtras.ie; one-off payment for MyAddress.ie (previously NewAddress.ie).

Website description:
MyAddress.ie enables people moving house to notify utility companies, banks and other institutions in one step. MovieExtras.ie is an online database of movie extras working, or available for work, in the Irish film and television industries. MovieExtras.ie provides search features to casting directors on a large database of movie extras.

Figure 8.2: MovieExtras.ie

Figure 8.3: NewAddress.ie

How / when did you decide to set up on your own?

I set up in 2002. I left industry in 2000. I worked in telecoms in eircom prior to that. I started working on a business idea. I worked on a business plan and tried to get funding for it for €1m. It didn't work!

Around this time, I teamed up with one of my business partners - Kevin Gill – who I knew through his wife. We spoke about a number of different projects. I came up with the idea for MovieExtras when I was sitting in the office and heard an ad for the movie *Veronica Guerin*. Everyone had to queue for hours to get screened. I thought it would be very suited to the Internet. When I got together with Kevin, we looked at a few ideas and MovieExtras was the cheapest! I then did some research abroad – there were some scam US sites in the area, and there's a similar one now in Ireland, but there was nothing quite like MovieExtras. I sat down and researched it all and estimated costs for it - €10,000 was my figure, much of it marketing. Kevin is technical and was able to build the site himself. Later we got a quote for the site that came in at €25,000 – we were able to save that with Kevin doing it for us. The site includes good search capability, contact and extras management system.

Were you always an entrepreneurial spirit?

YES! I always wanted to do something. I was selling at seven years old. The owner of Smart Bros suits lived across the road. I asked for hangers, he gave me a sack of them, and I then sold them door-to-door.

Which came first? MovieExtras or NewAddress?

MovieExtras was first in September 2002. In 2004, while Kevin went away for two weeks, things were really quiet and I got bored! I did up a slide on moving address – and that started NewAddress. MovieExtras was ongoing and around this time we brought in a salesperson and also someone to manage MovieExtras and get it more involved with productions directly.

How did it come about?
When I decided to leave work, I didn't have an idea for a business yet. I had a job in eircom at the time, and I was holding out for a new job I was hoping to get in Stockholm where I'd be consulting, earning lots of money. Finally, the new job said 'No'. That day, I went home and figured 'OK, that's that … I'm working in eircom'. But next day, I went straight to the marketing officer and said I was resigning. I was ready to start something on my own.

How much money was required to set up your businesses? How did you go about funding NewAddress (and MovieExtras)?
For MovieExtras, my partner Kevin built the site and not much money was required. With NewAddress, a lot of work needed to happen in the background before we could launch. We needed to get the banks and institutions on board to accept the address changes coming from us. We applied and got funding through Enterprise Ireland – through the HotHouse programme. It was a fantastic programme, of huge assistance to us. The main benefits were that you were sitting around with other like-minded people – a really positive environment. Also the course directors were able to introduce us to a great network of people. Before launch, MyHome.ie expressed an interest and we sat down with them – they invested before launch.

How did you have your first website developed? What did it cost?
Our recent version of MovieExtras required a young, fresh, filmy look and feel and we spent €2,500 on the logo and branding design. For NewAddress, we needed a strong corporate brand that people would trust. We got graphic design quotes coming in at €25,000, €10,000, €4,000 (just for graphic design). Our brand needed to be trustworthy, reliable, and corporate. We took a high end quote, and didn't regret it.

NewAddress is a one-off fee paid by the person moving, and MovieExtras is an annual subscription fee. What differences do you see between the two?
Overall, MovieExtras is doing better but New Address has better long term possibilities.

Was purchase from a third party part of your initial business plan?
Yes. Three to five years to sell on to a third party.

Being an entrepreneur, have you any new ideas on the go?
Yes – lots! One is CastingZone.ie – a site for actors, models and crew, rather than extras.

What marketing methods do you use for your websites? PR? Newsletters? Pay-per-click? Print ads? Web portals?
There are two big differences – NewAddress is a service, whereas on MovieExtras, the expectation is to get work. MovieExtras is more like a broker. With MovieExtras, we are limited in how many people we can take on before the database gets unwieldy – we manage individual projects ourselves manually. So we keep marketing low-key to stop the database getting too big. All people are personally selected and passed on for jobs as most suitable. Our current database has about 2,500 in it, but we may raise that to 4,000 next year in accordance with jobs coming down the line.

What have been the highpoints, and lowpoints, of running your own business?
High has definitely been the satisfaction of doing it. I have other initiatives on the go, such as Fundraisingboxes.ie, etc. and the satisfaction for me has always been in seeing my ideas get off the ground. Fundraisingboxes.ie came about when I was working with Club100 helping to raise money. We had students collecting for us and had to make sure we weren't ripped off and so we needed tamper-evident boxes. There were none in Ireland, so I brought them in and

personalised them. We raised €5,000 and bought St. Michael's House a mini-bus. Next thing I know, St. Luke's called with an order. So it went from there. It's not a huge business but it's there and it's working. There is great satisfaction out of something like that.

Both of your websites have a national audience and customer-base. Do you think either of them could have succeeded in a non-Internet environment?

No. The cost for doing a paper based model for NewAddress would have been exorbitant and wouldn't have delivered the ease-of-use to the end-customer. Both sites were classic Internet models – lots of entities on both sides, a middle-man needed in between – perfect for the Internet. For MovieExtras, a person in Kerry now has equal access to nationwide jobs as someone in Dublin, without having to track down and travel for every audition.

What are the advantages of working for yourself against working for someone else?

I work harder, but it's absolutely brilliant. At times, I have put in 70 / 80 hours a week but it's worth it.

Of your various business ventures, what are you most proud of?

Money received and paid out in wages! Hearing stories of happy customers. We had one lady, aged 84, whose photo was used on a billboard via MovieExtras and she was thrilled. We had another lady whose birthday it was, and always wanted to be an extra on the Fair City set, which we were able to make happen. One thing that's lovely about MovieExtras is that we've enabled people who are not in the 'in' circle to have access to jobs and opportunities they wouldn't have otherwise. That's a great feeling.

What would you like to do for the future?

I want to keep developing new businesses. It's not so much about them being successful but about doing them.

Any other advice you'd like to share?
One thing I'd like to say is that people are very helpful if you ask. Pick up the phone and ask, no matter who they are.

What would you say to someone starting out?
START! Lots of people talk about it but don't follow up.

What websites do you like and admire?
Polldaddy – check for online polls; StatCounter; Daft; and Iflow.ie.

8.3 EAMONN FALLON, CO-CEO, DAFT.IE

Figure 8.4: Daft.ie

Online business type:
Property portal, suppliers pay to advertise.

Website description:
Daft is Ireland's largest property website, for sales and lettings. Approximately nine out of every 10 properties for sale in Ireland are advertised on Daft. In 2007, over €60 billion of property was sold through Daft and over €1.1 billion in rent was collected.

Have you always been an entrepreneurial spirit? Was Daft.ie your first venture on your own / with family?
I have always been interested in building new things and was very lucky that my parents very much encouraged this. When I was in college, I helped my father set up a software company called Floorcad, where we developed a software package that is now used by concrete flooring manufacturers in about 30 different countries around the world. Recently, he just came back from a trip to Iraq, where it looks like he will gain a new customer in Kurdistan, which is one of the areas in the world where the building industry is still booming.

When I left college in 1999, I went to work for a very entrepreneurial guy called Eddie Murphy, who ran an Internet design company called Labyrinth. It was a relatively large company, compared to other internet design companies around at the time, and had about 50 employees. It was an exciting place to work as most of the staff were in their 20s and Eddie gave us a lot of responsibility. I remember going on a trip to London with him and his business partner, where we pitched the CTO of Royal Bank of Scotland on a product to do dynamic currency conversion over the Internet. We didn't win the business but, as a 20-year old getting the chance to pitch to senior people in huge companies, this really opened my eyes to the world of business. From that meeting, the product idea grew and I left Labyrinth in 2000 to join Eddie's new company, Global Currency Exchange, as the first employee. The company is now hugely successful and processes hundreds of millions of credit card payments from many of the world's low cost airlines, including Ryanair.

Throughout all this time, I was still involved in Daft with my brother Brian and eventually left paid employment in 2003 to run

Daft.ie fulltime, as I could see from working with Eddie how rewarding it can be to own and run your own company.

How / when did you decide to set up on your own?
The idea for Daft came about around the family dinner table in 1997. My sister had just finished college and was looking to rent an apartment in town with a friend. She was complaining about how annoying it was to use the local evening paper, the *Evening Herald*, to find a place to live. By the time she finished work, a lot of the ads were out-of-date as they had already been let earlier that day. Many of the places that were available were totally unsuitable when she visited them, as there was no real way of knowing what a place was like from a two-line ad with no photographs or proper addresses. Two months beforehand, we had just signed up to Ireland's first affordable consumer Internet offering from Indigo, which gave Internet access for only IR£25 a year. Naturally, we just assumed that there would be a website out there that would list properties for sale and to let. Ideally, the website would include photos along with the full address and, when they were sold or let, the advertiser would take them down so as not to waste the time of people looking. An intensive search on AltaVista (Google hadn't been launched yet) yielded no results and we realised that we were the first people to come up with the admittedly obvious idea of a property website.

Myself and Brian did some brainstorming and came up with the name Daft as we wanted a fresh Internet-sounding name like 'Yahoo' and not a boring generic name like 'HomesOnline' or 'PropertyNet', etc. A few weeks later, Brian sat down and developed the very first rudimentary version of Daft.ie and launched it at the not-so-easy-to-remember URL of www.indigo.ie/~briann. A year later, we got the daft.ie domain and a year after that we went nationwide.

Did you use your own money, or receive any funding or financial assistance from friends and family?
It didn't cost very much to set up Daft, just time and effort. However, when the website really started taking off in 2000, we got a loan from our dad of IR£12,000 to buy servers and hosting, which we needed to keep up with the user demand. We paid it back in full two years later.

Did you receive any funding from Enterprise Boards or financial institutions? If yes, did you find it hard to secure that funding?
To be honest, I really hate paper-work and form-filling, so we stayed well clear of the government agencies whom we thought would just waste our time with pointless feasibility studies. However, things have gotten a lot better since we started and I would recommend anyone starting a business now to talk to their local Enterprise Board.

What option did you choose for getting your first website built? An Irish web house, foreign developers, independent developer or build yourself?
We built everything ourselves, which is why we didn't really need any funding.

I can see you've done a re-launch of your existing website – well done – it looks cleaner and professional. How has it evolved from your first website?
We now have a team of six developers, who look after all aspects of developing and running our sites. We have gone through about five major iterations of the site since we launched in 1998, and the latest one is our fastest and most efficient yet. Having gone from a few hundred unique visitors per month back in 1998 to over 1.2 million per month in 2009, a lot of our time is spent making sure all those people have an easy-to-use, enjoyable experience and delivering them the results they want in as short a time as possible.

Who did you get to do your current website – a website house?

Our approach to web design is very scientific and we spent a lot of time in the research phase of our current design. The process for the current design took about six months and we started out by taking screenshots of the 100 or so different pages that are used on the site and went through each one asking ourselves 'How do we make this page clearer and easier-to-use?'. We then produced wireframes of each new page, deciding exactly what text and user functions would appear on various parts of the page. It was only at this stage that we brought in an external graphic designer who took our wireframes and added that extra polish.

What costs were involved in setting up the website?

A website can be built very cheaply if you are willing to put in a lot of work yourself. If you know a good designer, and you do all the thinking yourself about the UI (user interface) design and the programming, you should be able to get a site up and running for less than €2,000. We do all the programming and UI design in-house and outsource the graphic design to one of our external freelancers. However, if you don't know any designers, there are great resources on the internet to source design talent – for example, **crowdspring.com**.

What additional costs were involved in setting up online at the beginning?

Because our traffic was low at the beginning, we used shared hosting, which cost just a few dollars per month. Now our hosting costs are in the tens of thousands, but that's because we are a high-traffic site.

Did you work from home to start with? Full-time or part-time?

When I left full-time employment in 2003, I worked from home to keep costs down but moved into a single office in the Digital Hub on Thomas Street after about six months. Enterprise spaces like the Digital Hub are great for start-ups, not because they are cheaper than standard commercial space, but because you get a flexible month-to-month lease. This allowed us to relocate within the hub many times, as we moved from one employee to 20.

What size is your premises now?
We moved out of the Hub in 2006, as we were spread across three floors in an old Georgian building. We moved to a 3,000 sq ft open plan office in Latin Hall on Golden Lane, which was a huge boost for productivity as it cut out a lot of trips up and down stairs!

How many staff do you have?
We now have 30 people on the team.

How many users do you have?
In May 2008, we attracted 1.2 million unique visitors, who generated 103 million page views. Out of all the property searches conducted online in Ireland, over 70% of them hit one of our sites (**daft.ie, rent.ie, property.ie, let.ie** and **daft.com**).

I see that after several years in business, you took your first steps to becoming serial entrepreneurs and you now also own Property.ie and Rent.ie. How are they developing in comparison to the behemoth that is Daft?
Our strategy with our other sites – rent.ie, property.ie and let.ie – is really about extending the lead we have over our other online competitors. We realise that, when people look online for property, many of them check more than one site. If people are going to look at a site other than Daft for property, we want them to use one of our sites instead of a competitor's. This is very much like the Procter & Gamble strategy with washing powder. When we bought property.ie in 2008, we had a 250% lead in terms of total audience over the number two site, myhome.ie. The top four websites at the time for property were daft.ie (1), myhome.ie (2), propertynews.com (3) and let.ie (4). In 2009, Daft now has a 300% lead over the number two and the top four sites

are www.daft.ie (1), property.ie / myhome.ie (2), rent.ie (3), let.ie / propertynews.com (4). This has allowed us to increase our market share of online property searches to over 70%.

How is Daft.com getting on with the Northern Ireland market? What, if any, differences have you seen in dealing with the UK rather than Irish market?

Our experience of Northern Ireland market has been very positive. We soft-launched daft.com into the marketplace in Q2 2009 and we already have over 20% of the Northern Ireland property market listed on the site. Northern Ireland estate agents are very receptive to our offering and welcome the competition to the existing players. We now have four people on the Northern Ireland team and are still hiring, as we are aiming to get over 50% of the market by Q2 2010.

Last year, you invested in Boards.ie and Adverts.ie. Boards.ie in particular is a well-known brand and heavily-visited site – and the primary business model seems to be pay-per-click ads. Are there any other plans to develop either of these sites further that you can tell us about?

Boards.ie is a very interesting investment for us. It attracts even more people every month than Daft.ie and provides a platform for the many special interest groups that exist in Ireland. For example, if you are into triathlons, you will find most of them are in the boards.ie cycling and triathlon forums. Many Leaving Cert students come onto the Leaving Cert forums to talk about papers and grinds, etc. The story about last year's leaked English paper broke first on boards.ie. We think that this kind of platform is a lot more powerful than traditional top-down media and will only increase in importance over the coming years. We have three sources of revenue for boards.ie:

- **Targeted display advertising:** For example, if colleges are trying to attract students to join their colleges, I can't think of any better place to advertise than in the boards.ie Leaving Cert forum;

- **Subscriptions:** For €50 per year, you can upgrade your account to a subscriber account. This gives you benefits like a custom profile, picture and personal blog space.

- **Talk-to forums:** Companies can buy a forum that allows them to talk directly to the boards.ie audience. Companies like Vodafone, Magnet and Richer Sounds are all doing it. It allows them to put a human face to their companies and to solicit detailed feedback on their product offerings. Magnet even launched a brand new broadband service, optimised for online gaming, based on feedback it received on the Magnet talk-to forum.

What do you see as Daft's ongoing Unique Selling Point?

Our unique selling point for advertisers is that we have by far the largest audience for property in Ireland and we provide the best return on investment for them *versus* newspapers or other online services. For property-hunters, our USP is that we have at least three times the number of properties listed compared to other online services and we have magnitudes more than the local and national newspapers. For example, if we were to publish a paper-based weekly property supplement, it would have over 10,000 pages!

Have you other contender competitors beyond MyHome.ie online?

We handle over 70% of all online property searches, so we really see our main competitors to be the national and local newspapers around Ireland. The recession actually is helping us in this battle, as people cannot afford to pay the exorbitant prices for print advertising anymore and are switching to cheaper online advertising that gives them a much better return on investment.

What shopping cart software do you use? Which payment gateway?

We have been satisfied customers of Realex payments for the last five years and process all our direct debit and credit card business through them.

What marketing methods do you use for your websites? PR? Newsletters? Pay-per-click? Print ads? Web portals? Tradeshows?
We have found that the most effective marketing method for driving traffic to our website is online advertising. Print doesn't work and TV and radio are very expensive. We have long term advertising contracts with ebay.ie and eircom.net. We also buy a lot of advertising from Google and Facebook. Tradeshows are a waste of time and not an efficient use of your marketing budget or time. PR works very well, but takes a lot of time and effort; an example of this is the Daft report. This works because we invest a lot in the production of high quality economic research and typically get blanket coverage by blogs, TV, radio, national and local press. However, the best form of marketing is word-of-mouth and this can only be achieved by having a great product that people want to talk about.

Do you find your blog effective in capturing extra hits and prospective customers?
We really just use our blog to put a human face on our company and use it as a communications channel to talk to our existing customers. However, I have heard of many success stories of people attracting new customers through their blog, especially for people selling physical products online like puddleducks.ie for children's clothes and curiouswines.ie for wine.

What websites do you like and admire?
I think Ger and Fred have done a really great job over at donedeal.ie.

Lastly, have you any words of advice for people considering setting up their own business?
Don't be afraid to talk to as many people as possible about your idea. I've never met anyone who has had an idea stolen, but I've met many people who've been too paranoid to talk about their idea and ended up never getting it off the ground. Also don't bother your time with lengthy business plans. Just write down three goals that you could achieve in

one year and get started. Finally, be ready for a lot of work and try to get a business partner on board as it can be very difficult to go it alone.

8.4 MAEBH COLLINS, THENATURALBABYRESOURCE.COM & BABAME.COM

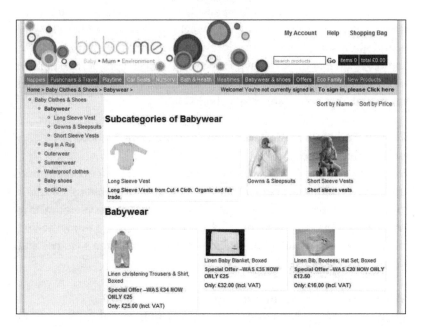

Figure 8.5: Babame.com

Online business type:

Online retailer, wholesaler, bricks-and-mortar shop-owner.

Website description:

TheNaturalBabyResource.com: Online retailer providing eco-friendly and natural products for babies, children and parents.

Have you always been an entrepreneurial spirit, even before TheNaturalBabyResource?

No! I was a chartered accountant, in corporate tax, but wasn't an entrepreneur. I just realised I hated it and wanted to do anything else.

Have you started any other ventures since then?

Yes, we have. Not long after launching the NBR shop, I realised that there was nothing stopping anyone else setting up a rival site to ours. To help protect that, we started a wholesale business selling eco-friendly nappies. We secured the nationwide trade licence for a nappy called BumGenius. Then the manufacturers asked us to take on all of Europe. This brand of nappy subsequently became the #1 worldwide eco-nappy and has particularly taken off in the last two years. So, we have a retail shop selling eco-friendly nappies, and we own the rights to distribute the #1 selling nappy in that market, too.

After three years, we took on our first bricks-and-mortar shop premises. We opened at the same time as we moved to our first warehouse of 2,000 sq ft. Recently, we launched into manufacturing for the first time with a set of breast-feeding support products. This is a new venture for us, but feedback so far is very positive. I'm really enjoying it.

How / when did you decide to set up on your own?

I started when I was pregnant and still working. At first, it was a hobby. I launched my first site during pregnancy and while I was still working in KPMG. The whole thing cost IR£100. I did the website myself using an online sitebuilder – it was very basic. That IR£100 included my first set of stock, too! My philosophy was to start with small amounts of stock, test it online and build more stock as we sold more. I believe in always growing organically. At the end of my maternity leave, I didn't go back. It was a risk at the time and we were touch-and-go for a while, but it was the right decision.

Did you work from home to start with? Full-time or part-time?
I started the business within our 3-roomed cottage, which already housed two adults, two kids, one on the way, and just one bedroom. We moved to a bigger house but, after a short time, there was stock in the shower, under the table, under the bed. One evening, my husband came home and quite literally could not get through the door! That was when we said we had to find premises. We got our first commercial premises of 1,000 sq ft after two years. It seemed huge, far too big. Within a year, we moved to our next premises, which was twice the size. After another year, we put a floor over much of the warehouse floor to create a section for offices. We have recently taken on three more units nearby to give us another 3,600 sq ft of warehouse space. I'm proud to say we have doubled turnover every single year, so the space has grown alongside that.

How has the recession hit you?
Of late, we have found business in Ireland very poor. We have turned our attention instead to the European wholesale business and the UK for the last while. We are going back to heavily discounted products, and back to nature to bring organic natural products to the market. We've gone back to strengths and our Unique Selling Potential.

Did you use your own money, or receive any funding or financial assistance from friends and family?
No, we grew organically from that first IR£100. We have no debts and no investors.

What option did you choose for getting your first website built? An Irish web house, foreign developers, independent developer or build yourself?
I used a basic and easy-to-use web-editor to build it myself. I had no prior computer training or knowledge beyond what I learned through accounting. It took me a week to make. I started out using PayPal as my payment gateway. I did get quotes from agencies but the cheapest

quote that came in was IR£10,000. I just thought "I'm not spending money on a site if I don't know if it will sell". That's been my approach all along. Don't go wild, take it steady, watch your costs. My accountancy background probably has something to do with it!

Who did you get to do your current website – website house / yourself, etc.?
I now use a company called NetSuite for our backend shop software and the look and feel (front end) of the current website was €5,000. We license the back end shopping and stock management software for €3,000 per annum. We find it great. When deliveries come in, the invoices are scanned and the stock is automatically updated. Our admin staff add new products to the site. We have 2,000+ up there now.

As a female entrepreneur, and mother, who started your business while pregnant – how have you found juggling motherhood and running your own business?
I have four children now. Running my own business makes it easier. I have no crazy commutes. If one of the kids is sick, I can take a day off. I do work a lot more! But it's easier overall. My husband works for the business now too, so between us we can work it out.

How many staff do you have now?
Twelve.

What is your Unique Selling Point over your competitors?
For TheNaturalBabyResource, it's simply that we're natural, and we have the biggest selection. We have a good price point, but we don't really compete on price. Not many are doing what we do in Ireland, but more mainstream shops are moving in; the market is moving towards this now. There are more sites setting up. This is good and bad for us – the awareness is good for our wholesale business, but bad for our retail. We realised early on that any retail site can be copied

unless we manufacture or trade wholesale. We've had instances of competitors contacting our distributor literally minutes after we launch a new product onto NBR. We realised we needed to trade to protect us. We also always try to innovate and stay ahead with new products.

What is the geographical distribution of your customer base?
Currently 50:50 retail UK / IRL. Most of our trade customers are in Europe and we now have French, German, Spanish, Portuguese and Polish speakers working for us – we have become more pan-European. Everyone who joins the company now needs to have a second language.

Which do you enjoy most – retail, trade, manufacturing?
Each day is a different answer. I love the variation.

What marketing methods do you use for your websites? PR? Newsletters? Pay-per-click? Print ads? Web portals? Tradeshows?
We now pay a PR person for us, who next week has set up meetings with every marketing manager in baby or parenting magazines in the UK. We also have a 'talk' person, who manages and updates our Facebook, Twitter and blog pages – we've just recently launched these. We've also done a print catalogue in the past, and we are back doing it again this year. It really has impact. We have 20,000 people on our database. The catalogues will cost €1 each but generate a huge buzz of orders when they arrive on the doormat. But, still, our best value for money for marketing is Google.

Lastly, have you any words of advice for people considering setting up their own business?
Don't compete on price only, you'll never do it. Go little by little. Don't try and take over the world. Grow organically. Avoid debt. When you make mistakes, make sure that they're ones you can afford.

8.5 KIERAN MURPHY, OWNER, ICECREAMIRELAND.COM

Figure 8.6: IceCreamIreland.com

Online business type:
Blog; has also written a book as a result of his blog.

Website description:
IceCreamIreland.com is the blog of an Irish ice-cream man in Dingle, Ireland with recipes of cookies, ice cream, and tips about everything from coffee to decoration included.

Did you set up your bricks-and-mortar business before you set up your blog?

Yes, we started Murphy's Ice Cream in 2000, many years before the blog!

How / when did you decide to set up your blog?
I started the blog in 2006. I had been thinking of doing it for a while and had a bit of spare time while on holiday in Morocco.

What was your initial goal in doing so?
There were three goals, really. The first was to create a stronger on-line presence to help with general marketing. The second was that we'd been asked so many times for recipes, and the third was to create an on-line space to keep in contact with customers.

Did you build the blog yourself?
Yes. I started it on Blogger, and then I switched to WordPress and my own domain.

How has the blog helped your bricks-and-mortar business, and vice versa?
The blog has helped by generating a lot of press (both from winning awards and from journalists finding it as part of online searches), by attracting the notice of a publisher (which led to the publication of our recipe book, *The Book of Sweet Things*) and by attracting customers. The business does boost the blog as well, since people who have eaten our ice cream find it if they want to know more about us.

You've recently brought out a book - is this a direct result of the IceCreamIreland blog? Tell us how that came about.
The commissioning editor at the time for Mercier Press was a customer, and he looked up the blog after it won at the Irish Blog Awards. He then contacted me and suggested I submit a proposal, which was accepted. In some ways, a blog is a perfect entry to the publishing world, since publishers can have a very concrete idea of

how you write and also know that there is a certain number of books that will be sold to the readers of a blog.

What marketing methods do you use for your websites? PR? Newsletters? Pay-per-click? Print ads? Web portals?
None of the above. We haven't felt the need to. I think the best marketing on-line is to interact with other people on-line.

What has helped to set you apart from other similar blogs?
At the time I started, most of the blogs in Ireland were technical, so having one about ice-cream attracted attention. Besides that, I think the photography really helps when it comes to food. If it looks tasty, you're more likely to gain readers.

What are the advantages of working for yourself against working for someone else?
You have more freedom to try to implement a vision, and the only people who can tell you what to do are your customers.

Any other advice you'd like to add?
It's a good idea to know what you want out of a blog before you start. You also should be passionate about your subject.

8.6 AODHÁN CULLEN, CEO, STATCOUNTER.COM

Online business type:
Direct download of free software; revenue from ad and upgrades.

Web business description:
StatCounter is a free invisible web-tracker, highly-configurable hit-counter and real-time detailed web statistics provider, with over two million users worldwide.

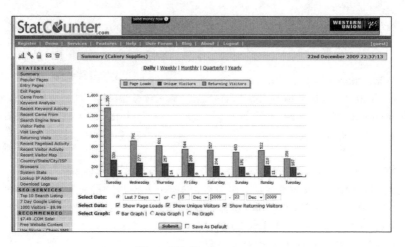

Figure 8.7: StatCounter.com

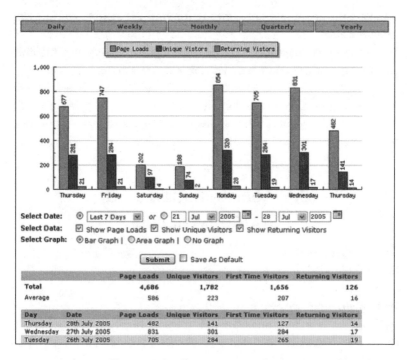

Figure 8.8: StatCounter.com sample report

While I know you started StatCounter at a very young age, were you an entrepreneurial spirit even before that?
I've been running businesses of various kinds from the age of 12 when I set up a CV-typing business. In my teens, I dabbled in website design. It was this experience that sowed the seeds for StatCounter. One customer said: "The website is fantastic – thanks, Aodhán. But is anyone actually visiting it?". In response to this question, which was repeatedly asked by my web design clients, I decided to set up StatCounter.

Did you use your own money, or receive any funding or financial assistance from friends and family?
It was all self-funded. That's what is great about an Internet business – there are very few financial barriers to entry. Subsequently every penny I made, I ploughed back into the business to expand and improve the service. At 16, though, I did have to borrow my Dad's credit card to pay for server hosting. I had the cash to pay the bill, but I couldn't get a credit card myself until 18!

Did you receive any funding at any stage from Enterprise Boards or financial institutions? If yes, did you find it hard to secure that funding?
No.

What option did you choose for getting your websites built? An Irish web house, foreign developers, independent developer or build yourself?
I built the first one myself, and we keep all development in-house today, too.

What additional set up costs were involved in setting up online?
Very few – I built the site myself, and worked from home for the first seven years. When you don't have financing and you're offering a free service, it's very important to keep costs low. I worked part-time on

the business while in school / college (although my college attendance record may not have been 100%) and then moved to full-time as soon as I did my final exams.

What size is your premises now?
We still run quite a small office – we have space in the Guinness Enterprise Centre. This is because many of the staff / contractors work remotely over the Internet. I have worked with some people for years, but never met them face-to-face.

How many staff do you have?
We've nine in total on the team now.

How many users do you have?
At this point, over 2 million.

How have you found competing with the behemoth competitor that is Google?
StatCounter was actually around for a few years before Google. We just continue to provide the best service possible.

What is your Unique Selling Point? What do you offer that Google Analytics does not?
The differences are:

- StatCounter is real-time – stats are available instantly, whereas they are 'lagged' or delayed for up to 24 hours with Google Analytics;
- StatCounter tracks BOTH JavaScript and non-JavaScript visitors; Google only tracks JavaScript visitors, so generally StatCounter tracks more visitors than GA; StatCounter provides individual visitor detail down to IP address level;
- StatCounter offers full customer support for help with installation and queries;

StatCounter provides you with the EXACT search terms being used to find your site.

We also hear that many of our members find our interface clearer and more intuitive than Google Analytics.

Are host providers' own statistics packages another competitor for you?
Not really. Many of these stats are based on raw server logs instead of real online visitors (the server logs include bot and crawler activity, which most people are not very interested in – a crawler is not going to purchase anything on your site!). Also, as the stats are presented in their raw form, they can be difficult to interpret; at StatCounter, we process all the stats into an easily understandable form. Further, we provide real-time stats so you can see what is happening on your site instantly. Many host provided stats are delayed by several hours, meaning there is a disconnect between what is happening on your site and you finding out about it.

What is the geographical distribution of your customer base?
40% US; 9% UK; 5% Canada; 4% India; 3% Australia, with the remaining 39% are located all over the world in many different countries.

What challenges do you face having a software download as your product, rather than a tangible one such as a book or DVD?
We don't really face any challenges compared to sellers of tangible goods – rather we have advantages, since we don't have physical storage or posting costs.

Your business model is currently based on pay-per-click advertising and upgrades from the basic StatCounter software to higher levels of service for greater pageloads. Do you see that changing at any point?
No!

Given that the majority of your customers are in the USA, do you host your servers there?
Yes.

What shopping cart software do you use? Which payment gateway?
Realex and PayPal.

What marketing methods do you use for your websites? PR? Newsletters? Pay-per-click? Print ads? Web portals? Tradeshows?
Word-of-mouth and PR. In fact, we grew to a membership base of over 1.5 million based on word-of-mouth alone. It's only in recent times that we have engaged a PR agent, to help us reach an even wider audience.

Do you find your blog effective in capturing extra hits and prospective customers?
The main use of our blog is to communicate with our members. We allow and encourage comments on all our blog posts, as we find it a very effective way of hearing comments and feedback. A by-product of this is that we can, and do, gain members who like what they see on the blog.

Lastly, have you any words of advice for people considering setting up their own business?
Have a very clear vision about what it is you want to achieve ... and then get up and do it! Sitting around talking about it never got a business off the ground.

9

RESOURCES

9.1 WEB RESOURCES

Courses on website design
www.enterpriseboards.ie

Domain name registries – checking whether your preferred domain name is available
http://www.whois.net – for .com and other names
http://www.whoislookup.ie/ - for .ie names

Financing
www.enterpriseboards.ie

Free directories to register your website with
www.browseireland.com
www.dmoz.org
www.finditireland.com
www.irish-guide.com

Hiring a developer online
www.freelancer.com
www.nixers.com
www.rentacoder.com

Irish .ie domain rules
http://www.iedr.ie – Irish Internet Domain Registry information

Irish website host providers (IHPs)
www.blacknight.com
www.myhost.ie
www.irishhosting.net
www.letshost.ie
www.register.ie
www.webworld.ie

Learn how to build your website yourself
http://build-website.com/

Payment providers for processing online credit / debit cards
www.2Checkout.com
www.datacash.com
www.paypal.com
www.realexpayments.com
www.rbsworldpay.com
www.worldnettps.com

Registering your company name
www.cro.ie

Shopping cart software
www.candypress.com – I use this – minimal charge – Windows-based.
www.oscommerce.com – Unix based but runs on Windows also – free
www.Zen-cart.com – Windows based, free

Website builders (included with host providers)
www.blacknight.com
www.darklite.ie
www.irishdomains.com
www.letshost.ie
www.myweb.ie

www.simplehosting.ie

Website builders (standalone)
sitebuilder.yahoo.com – free

Website development houses - Irish
www.continuum.ie
www.iworks.ie
www.stormweb.ie
www.webfactory.ie
www.webtrade.ie

Website editors
sharepoint.microsoft.com
www.adobe.com/products/dreamweaver/
www.kompozer.net (free, open source)

Website template websites – Download and modify
www.templatefactory.com
www.templatemonster.com
www.websitetemplates.com

9.2 EXAMPLE WEBSITES FOR DIFFERENT BUSINESS MODELS

Blogs
www.twentymajor.net – thoughts and musings of a Dublin man
www.beaut.ie – two Irish women covering all topics on latest beauty products, make up, fashion.
www.huffingtonpost.com
www.icecreamireland.com – blog of the owner of IceCreamIreland shop
www.perezhilton.com – celebrity and Hollywood gossip

Blog software
www.blogger.com
www.typepad.com
www.wordpress.com

Message boards /chat forums
www.askaboutmoney.com
www.boards.ie – very popular, broad-reaching Irish online message board
www.cluas.com – for music fans
www.magicmum.com – mums of all kinds chatting
www.rollercoaster.ie – pregnancy and parenting

Online shops
www.cdwow.ie
www.craftsupplies.ie
www.diywedding.ie
www.hairybaby.com
www.thenaturalbabyresource.com

Portals
www.ireland.com – general news, travel, recently purchased myhome.ie
www.irishweddingsonline.com
www.myhome.ie – property portal
www.weddingsonline.ie

PR software – for distributing press releases
www.get2press.ie
www.medialive.com
www.przone.ie

Service
www.myaddress.ie

Social portals
www.bebo.com – social networking site popular with children and teenagers
www.facebook.com – as above, but tends to appeal to an older demographic
www.friendsreunited.co.uk – initially a site for helping old friends reunite, but now a popular dating site and also covers ancestry searches and other features

Subscriptions
www.movieextras.ie

9.3 WEB DEVELOPMENT LANGUAGES & TERMS*

HTML is the primary language used to develop code that works on the web.

XML is another, similar language, used for Internet development that has a little more power than HTML.

XSL is used to create cascading stylesheets, which are used to create templates for the look, feel and behaviour of a site. XSL effectively separates the content of a site from the look and feel of the site, allowing one to be modified without affecting the other.

Flash is also used to create dynamic, moving pages.

PHP is used to create scripts that enable actions and add more 'intelligence' to your web pages rather than just displaying content – for example, a 'Please Add Me to Your Newsletter' form, which then sends the customer's email address to you when they hit the 'submit' button.

* Please note these are my easy-to-digest definitions rather than formal ones!

9.4 TYPICAL REQUIREMENTS FOR A MERCHANT ACCOUNT APPLICATION

- Application form.
- Schedule of fees.
- Direct debit mandate (signed).
- Bank confirmation (a copy of a cheque from the business bank account or a copy of a bank statement or online bank statement).
- Proof of business existence, such as a utility bill or invoice addressed to the business at the business address.
- Identity and address verification for any signatory / signatories of the application.

If you are a partnership, you must provide a copy of your partnership agreement. If you are trading from a home address, you must provide a reference from your bank confirming you have had your business account in operation for the last six months and that they consider you trustworthy and reliable, though there are some exceptions from this requirement.

Website checklist
Your website must have the following displayed and accessible, either on a test site or on the main web page, before the bank will assess your application for an internet merchant account:

- Company name.
- Customer service telephone number or e-mail address.
- Refund and return policy.
- Listing of products, with pricing stated in the merchant settlement currency.
- Delivery methods and timing.

- Privacy policy.
- Terms and conditions, with a tick-box for the customer to tick to say they accept the terms.
- On the payment page, a box for the customer's CVV2 number to be entered.
- The delivery cost shown alongside the cost of the good(s), with a total charge also being shown.
- Card Association marks must be displayed – for example, Visa, MasterCard.
- Website order page is secure.
- The domain is registered to the merchant.

9.5 MY OWN SITES

Figure 9.1: Craftsupplies.ie

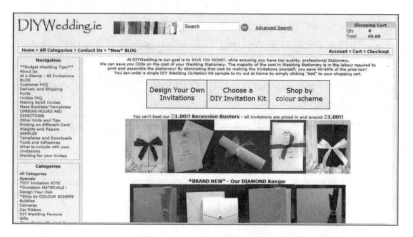

Figure 9.2: DIYwedding.ie

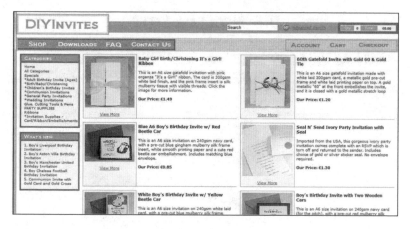

Figure 9.3: DIYinvites.ie

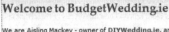

Welcome to BudgetWedding.ie

- Home
- Stationery
- The Dress
- Photography
- Bridesmaids
- Day Accessories
- The Venue
- Decorations
- Flowers
- Wedding Cakes
- Favours
- Green Weddings
- IKEA/ETSY
- Budget Tips
- Using the Internet
- DIY Checklist
- Supplier Directory
- DIYWedding Website

We are Aisling Mackey - owner of DIYWedding.ie, and Sarah Traynor - author of the book How to have a Champagne Wedding on a Bucks Fizz Budget. Our goal is to give you as much information, advice and tips as we can about how to maximise your wedding budget. If you have any tips you'd like to pass on yourself - please tell us!! Enjoy the site!

DIY Stationery has never been so easy!
Stationery is a great starting point for saving hundreds, if not thousands of Euros on your wedding. By making your own, you add a personal touch and save approx. 60% of the costs in the process! Learn how to eliminate expensive printing and labour costs by using the latest all-inclusive DIY kits to easily make your own fantastic invitations, RSVPs, Thank Yous and Mass Booklets.

Saving €00s on your Wedding Dress
Our Site co-author Sarah got married in 2004. She tried on

Figure 9.4: BudgetWedding.ie

10

GOOD LUCK!

So, we're at the end of the book. I hope you have learnt enough to start your own website. I look forward to seeing you online someday soon at **www.clickthrough.ie**.

In the meantime, remember what the entrepreneurs in our case studies said:

- If in doubt ... do it. Given the low cost of entry to setting up an Internet business, it is a rare person who regrets doing it.

- Setting up your own business isn't easy. You will always hit hurdles along the way. Of the six people I spoke with for these case studies, nearly all had tried other ventures before starting their current, successful one.

- Use the data at disposal in an online environment to its maximum capability to provide a content-rich, personalised, unique experience for the customer through your e-business.

- Never stop innovating. Cut off product lines that aren't selling well, introduce new ones and advertise through email to your customer base.

- Above all, enjoy it!

> *START!*
> *Lots of people talk about it but don't follow up.*
> **Derek Quinn,**
> *MovieExtras.ie and NewAddress.ie*

OTHER TITLES FROM OAK TREE PRESS

QUICK WIN MARKETING
Answers to your top 100 marketing questions
Annmarie Hanlon
€12.95 pb : ISBN 978-1-904887-78-2

QUICK WIN MARKETING is aimed at entrepreneurs and business managers wanting to start, grow or revitalise a business and companies launching new services or products in Ireland or the UK. It is full of practical hints, budget tips and checklists on new and traditional marketing tactics and is supported by a website: **www.quickwinmarketing.com**.

QUICK WIN DIGITAL MARKETING
Answers to your top 100 digital marketing questions
Annmarie Hanlon & Joanna Akins
€12.95 pb : ISBN: 978-1-904887-87-2

QUICK WIN DIGITAL MARKETING is aimed at entrepreneurs, business managers and marketing people seeking a practical approach to digital marketing. There are five sections to the book: Digital Essentials; Digital Toolbox; Digital Marketing; Branding Online; and Managing, Measuring and Making Money Online. You also can search for questions and answers across a range of topics: blogs / microblogs; email; mobile; photo / audio / video; social media; surveys and web.

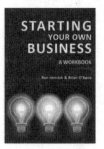

STARTING YOUR OWN BUSINESS:
A Workbook 3rd edition
Ron Immink & Brian O'Kane
€20 pb : ISBN 978-1-904887-35-5

Now in its **third** edition. Commissioned in 1997 by the Department of Enterprise, Trade and Employment to meet a real need for practical, relevant information among would-be entrepreneurs, **Starting Your Own Business: A Workbook** has been updated/expanded to reflect changing trends in Irish small business.

Available from good bookshops or www.oaktreepress.com